THE ART OF
FRESH &
DRIED FLOWER
ARRANGING

Mary Lawrence

PHOTOGRAPHY BY
Richard Paines

MAGNA
BOOKS

Published by Magna Books
Magna Road
Wigston
Leicester LE18 4ZH

Produced by Bison Books Ltd
Kimbolton House
117A Fulham Road
London SW3 6RL

ISBN 1-85422-442-5

Printed in Hong Kong

All flower arrangements are by Mary Lawrence and photographed by
Richard Payne, except the pictures as follows:

Additional photographic material: © Balthazar Korab: pages 15, 41, 93,
98-99, 110, 111, 113, 154, 155
New England Stock Photo: © Charley Freiberg: pages 126, 156; ©
Johnson Studio: page 100; © L. O'Shaughnessy: page 10; © Al Riccio:
pages 14, 69, 85, 115

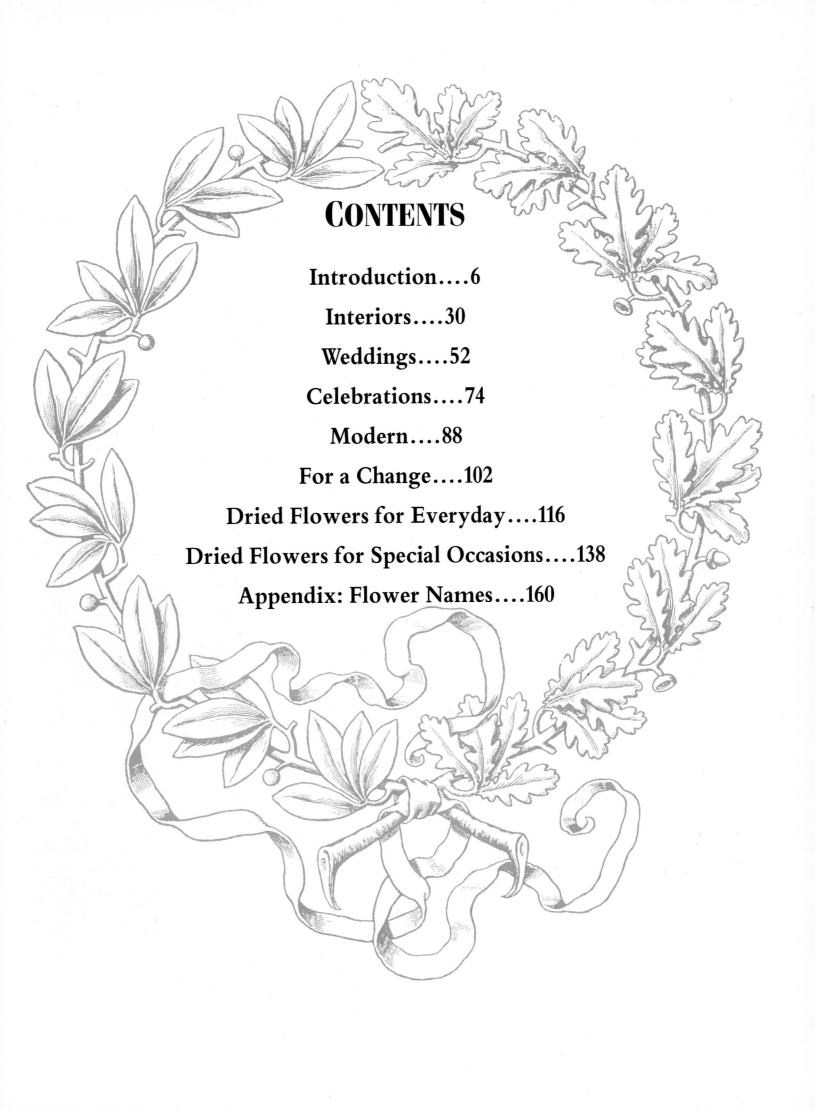

CONTENTS

INTRODUCTION

In the past hundred years the art of flower arranging has developed enormously in the West and has now attained a standing of some significance in both the amateur and professional spheres. In previous centuries, however, little was recorded about the Western style of flower arranging.

We know that the art of oriental flower arranging dates back to the sixth century BC. It was first developed in relation to Buddhist practice; in the Buddhist temple all the individual flowers and the line of the arrangement as a whole had a religious significance, and the art of flower arranging was considered a sacred rite. A search of the history books reveals further use of flowers. The wall paintings of ancient Egypt and Minoan Crete depicted terracotta vases filled with lotus flowers, and garlands and wreaths for the head containing forget-me-nots and buttercups. We know that the ancient Greeks used aromatic herbs and fragrant flowers woven together into garlands, which they wore for their festivals. The beautiful carved swags on early Roman buildings depicting flowers and foliage give a hint of flower arranging at that time. We also know that the Romans loved roses, regarding them as a symbol of love and wearing them as crowns at their feasts. They also used roses for their perfume, and would sleep on a fragrant bed of rose petals, or strew them through their rooms and walk on them.

In the fourteenth century there was considerable interest in rose gardens – again the rose was treasured as a symbol of the courtly love that inspired the poets of the day – and it is possible that roses were used to decorate the home at that time. The Renaissance period brought a tremendous interest both in gardens and in flowers as such. Explorers and travelers introduced flowers from the East into Europe and the paintings of the period feature these as well as roses and lilies, iris and violets.

The present day flower arranger owes much to the inspiration of the great Dutch and Flemish flower painters of the seventeenth century, Jan van Huysum, Jan Brueghel and Jan Davidsy. They were among the first artists to explore still life as a genre in its own right; their paintings show a massive abundance of glorious color and also particular, closely observed characteristics, such as a curving stem or tendril. They would use pale flowers to create a highlight against a dark flower, and also introduced fruit into their arrangements, or an ear of corn, globe artichoke or cabbage leaf, to give a variety of form and texture. Similarly, they used brambles, tree branches laden with fruit, or flowers past their best, even a seed head, to achieve the atmosphere they wanted. Everything from nature is depicted in their pictures, including insects, snails and birds' nests. These beautiful paintings will continue to be a source of inspiration to all people who enjoy and arrange flowers.

This low circular arrangement (left) is perfect for a large round table. The shallow bowl has been filled with wire netting which supports this all-round posy shape. The outline of mixed silver and purple foliage highlights the various shades of mauve flowers.
Plant materials: *Clematis, White Poplar, Silver Artemisia Purple Decorative Cabbage, Mauve Pansies, Astrantia, Button Spray Chrysanthemums.*

The Regency period saw a return to classical simplicity in the design of furniture, fashions and flowers, but the Victorian era produced a rich middle class which spent money on appearances, and suddenly flowers featured very much in the home. They became a pastime and almost a daily duty for the lady of the house. The lower classes, on the other hand, who could not afford the time or the luxury of flowers, were inclined to feel that flowers were rather unhealthy to have in the home. The typical middle-class Victorian room was very cluttered with heavy furniture and knick-knacks. The main feature was always a round table covered with a velvet cloth. On this would stand a round porcelain or silver bowl in which would be massed a group of flowers of mainly one color.

The Victorians created beautiful gardens for their grand houses and it was the head gardener's duty to grow and deliver suitable flowers for the house. He would also make corsages for the ladies to wear when attending their grand balls, and garlands to decorate the skirts of their dresses. The Victorians reintroduced the fashion of carrying flowers, first established in the sixteenth century to ward off germs and bad smells. They also created the language

In the imaginative world of a seventeenth-century Flemish painter, flowers of any season were painted together on the canvas. Particular detail was given to small dainty curling stems and stigmas, and fruit, vegetables and insects were all painted into the composition. These paintings have been a great inspiration to the flower arranging movement of the twentieth century. Here a wide variety of flowers have been arranged in the Flemish style. Plant materials: Dill, Hollyhocks, Asters, Roses, Japanese Anenomes, Canterbury Bells, Cornflowers, Thistle, Lavender, Mallow, Bells of Ireland, Ivy, Japonica, Clematis, Oak, Hops, Grapes, Quince, Crab Apples.

The addition of baby's breath lightens the single-flower arrangement.
Plant materials: *Marguerites,* *Gypsophila (Baby's Breath).*

This cheerful mix of garden flowers (right) has been informally arranged in a terracotta jug.
Plant materials: *Yellow Roses, Blue Scabius, Astrantia,* *Antirrhinum, Ivy, Hebe, Camomile, Japanese Anenome, Rosemary, Salvia, Queen Anne's Lace, Sneezewort.*

of flowers, so that the flowers carried in little nosegays by the ladies could also convey a very significant message.

The early settlers in North America grew flowers mainly for culinary and medicinal purposes. It was the Dutch settlers in New Amsterdam, bringing their native horticultural skills with them, who created beautiful orchards and flower gardens. When Williamsburg became the capital of Virginia, the inhabitants began to build suitably handsome and spacious wooden houses in the characteristic 'colonial' style, and beautiful gardens were created to match the newly elegant interiors. Besides the wealth of flowers brought in from other countries, there was a natural abundance of native flowers and foliages.

Paintings of the early eighteenth century show arrangements of flowers that contain carnations, pinks, ranunculus, foxgloves, roses, and the bulb flowers, irises, lilies, tulips and crown imperials. As the pace of exploration increased, new flower types became available from Mexico, South Africa and China, introducing brilliant colors and exotic scents. As the interest in flower arrangement flourished, it was inevitable that flower arrangements should become more massed and that each room should have not just one central arrangement but arrangements on every little table and mantelpiece. The whole effect must have been over-powering to the point of chaos. Toward the end of the nineteenth century, in reaction to this over-

A deceptively simple and gloriously colorful arrangement of soft sweet pea flower combined with airy gypsophila is enhanced by the matching bowl, and captures the essence of early summer.
Plant materials: *Sweet peas, Gypsophila.*

In this combination of wild and cultivated flowers in a rustic pot (above), the container lends informality to an otherwise formal arrangement.
Plant materials: *Red Roses, Alstroemeria, Button*

Chrysanthemums, September Weed, Italian Ruscus.

Single blossoms in individual containers (right) spaced on a long shelf or table for effect.
Plant materials: *Anthurium, Galax Leaves.*

14

abundance, single-flower arrangements became more stylish and a vogue, still noticeable today, developed for a dozen carnations and some fern.

The return to a simpler style was championed by John Ruskin and William Morris, inspirers of the Arts and Crafts Movement which responded to increasing industrialization by reasserting the value and importance of the individual hand-made object. One of the greatest influences of the twentieth century was that inspired flower gardener Gertrude Jekyll who, in her book *Flower Decorations in the Home* (1907), established many of the precepts central to flower arranging today, suggesting using crumpled wire to hold flowers in position and also encouraging the use of a wide variety of garden foliage.

After the Arts and Crafts trend in flower arranging there followed another period of change in the 1930s, when two flower arrangers of natural genius emerged. The American J. Gregory used the exotic blooms from North America and Mexico to create strong designs with dominant lines that accentuated the natural tendency of the blooms. He encouraged investigation of the Oriental tradition of flower arranging. The doyenne of the English flower arranging movement at this time was Constance Spry, who was inspired by seventeenth-century Flemish painting. Both these innovative designers believed that a flower arranger should look at the fine arts, which follow principles rather than rules and allow for full creative expression.

With the 1940s and world war came an inevitable but temporary decline in interest in flower arranging, but the end of the decade saw a flourishing growth in the flower industry. The speed of airfreight meant that flowers could be moved from any part of the world very quickly and the idea of seasonal flowers became a thing of the past. This growth in the flower industry led to a renewed interest in flower arranging and many flower clubs were formed in both America and Europe. The wives of American service men who had been stationed in Japan looked with excited interest at the Japanese style of flower arranging called

The long flowering period of lady's mantle makes it one of the most popular garden flowers to grow. Its lightness of form also makes it a flower arranger's delight for use as a filler or to soften an outline, or arranged on its own to demonstrate its dainty but dramatic qualities. The long neck of this container (right) comfortably supports the thin stems of the heavily flowered branches, while the luminous lime green of the blossom is repeated in the variegated glaze on this beautiful vase.
Plant material: *Lady's Mantle*

How welcoming to be greeted by this display (left) on a cold dismal day. This is an example of how warm colors appear to advance toward you.
Plant materials: *Antirrhinum, Alstroemeria, Spray Carnations, Honeysuckle, Plum branches.*

'Ikebana'. The study of Ikebana had been an essential part of Japanese culture since the arranging of flowers in harmony with the Buddhist temple came to be considered a sacred rite. Ikebana was concerned only with linear arrangements, as opposed to the massed floral decorations of the West, and used mainly branches and grasses, with just a few flowers. It was a complex and symbolic art form and many schools of flower arranging were founded, headed by masters who created rigid forms of symbolism. It takes many years of study to perfect the art of Ikebana. Ikebana International was formed in 1958 to stimulate the study and spread the art and there are now more than two hundred chapters in the world.

THE ART OF FLOWER ARRANGING

Flower arranging is not a technical exercise but an art form and requires no previous expertise other than knowledge of the basic elements of all art which are color, line and proportion.

COLOR

Color is the most striking element of any flower arrangement, but no two people perceive colors in the same way. The three primary colors are red, yellow and blue and the secondary colors are orange, green and violet. You can educate your eye into a good perception of color by standing in a garden in midsummer and looking at the different colors. You will quickly discover that most flowers are not examples of the pure primary and secondary colors but are hues and shades of these, either darker or lighter than the the main color. There are also very few pure white flowers; most have a tint of color in them.

Remember that, while black is the color of mourning in the Western world, white is used for mourning in Asiatic countries. In the past, red denoted danger because for primitive men it signified fire, but today it is considered a color of warmth. It is important to keep an open mind about color. The decision as to which color flowers to use to harmonize with the setting in which they are to be placed is a matter not of hard and fast rules but of individual taste. One other important aspect to remember when choosing flower colors for a room is that the warm colors depicted left appear to be advancing, whereas cool colors appear to recede.

The two principal types of color arrangements often referred to are 'polychromatic' and 'monochromatic'. 'Poly' means many and 'chroma' color (from the Latin), so obviously a polychromatic arrangement will consist of a mixture of colors, while a monochromatic one consists of flowers in many shades of one tint (page 8).

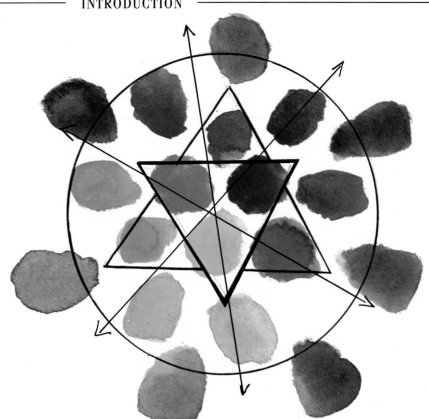

Excitement and interest is added to this arrangement (left) by the complete contrast of colors, shapes and textures. Dainty pale mauve freesias have been arranged in a triangular shape, which is broken by a sweep of orange-colored waxen lilies with markings that are matched in the famous Royal Lancastrian fire crystal glaze.
Plant materials: *Mauve Freesias, Lilium mid-century hybrid 'Enchantment'.*

The principal triangle in the color wheel (right) highlights the three primary colors, the subsidiary triangle the three secondary ones.

COLOR WHEEL

Most of us have an instinctive feel for the right mix of color: we know which colors go together, which colors clash, those that are warm and those that are cold. Perhaps we have not thought, however, that these intuitive feelings are founded on rigid scientific principles. You may remember from your school days that seemingly white daylight is made up of a spectrum of colors and that a glass prism will break this down into visible colors. You may even call to mind that little verse which was intended to help us remember these colors: 'Richard Of York Gave Battle In Vain', the first letters giving us Red, Orange, Yellow, Green, Blue, Indigo, Violet. Of these the red, yellow and blue are called primary colors because in painters' terms it is from these that all other colors can be made. The British scientist Sir Isaac Newton in the seventeenth century carried out experiments with a prism and produced what he called a color wheel to show the relationship of one color to the next. This was in effect a circle divided into segments, the dividing lines looking like spokes of a wheel.

This method of showing color relationship has since became standard. It was further developed by Moses Harris, a British engraver, who first published a detailed color wheel in 1776 in the style that we use today. Our color wheel shows the three *primary* colors and the three *secondary* colors, which are made up by mixing the primary colors on either side, giving orange, green, violet. In between these secondary and primary colors is a midway color mix. Although we have only shown one color at this position between the spokes of the triangles, the number of colors of course is infinite, depending on how near or far you move from the primary.

On the wheel, you will see that diametrically opposite each color segment is an opposite color, each warm color having its cool opposite and vice versa. Also each color has its *tint*, which is a mixture of that color and white, making it lighter. There are also *shades* where black is added, making it darker, and a *tone* where the addition is gray, thus making the color muted, but the relationship with the original colors in the color wheel still hold good. You will probably find the wheel very useful for occasional reference, and it should help in solving some of those problems of why certain colors are unhappy with others. It will also, however, help you plan some stunning, if less orthodox, combinations, for the subtle effect of a warm color against a cool one, as seen on left.

LINE

Line is the direction that the arrangement takes; it gives an emotional quality to the flower design. The vertical line, inspired by the soaring heights of Gothic architecture, is adopted when creating arrangements for narrow spaces where a tall erect style is dictated. The horizontal line is used on low flat surfaces, tables or mantelpieces, where the flower design will take a reclining shape. Curved lines are best used when the background is provided by a setting of soft, rounded lines of furniture. A combination of these different lines gives form to an arrangement; the basic forms are a pyramid, sphere, cube or cone, any of which are a suitable basic shape for a massed flower arrangement. When creating a massed arrangement, you must be very careful not to lose the three-dimensional aspect of the design.

Much can be learnt by a good appreciation of texture. Texture affords a pleasing variation and adds an extra dimension to any arrangement. Texture is abundant in nature; on a short country walk you will find cones, branches, dull and shiny leaves, seed heads and many other products of nature that can add an extra dimension to an arrangement. The strong shiny petals of the lily contrast with the soft feather bells of the freesia used in the arrangement on page 18, while the soft curly foliage of the tortured willow complements and highlights the striking lines of the white stock on page 68-69. Similar combinations can be seen in some of the other arrangements featured in this book. The hard outline of the artichokes have been softened by the texture of the carnations used on page 96, while the careful placing of ivy stems gathered on a country walk adds tremendous depth to the flower arrangement on page 11.

BALANCE

Balance is a very important element of any design. When arranging flowers, the grouping of the plant material must be in proportion to the container and give an overall pleasing effect. The weight of the arrangement as a whole should appear to be balanced from the angle of view. The composition of the flower design should have a rhythm that will lead the eye from the flowers to the setting, and leave an image that is remembered long after the flowers have died.

GATHERING FLOWERS

This section will be of little interest to an experienced flower arranger. However, it is included because the information is of paramount importance to somebody new to flower arranging. One of the greatest joys for the amateur flower arranger is to grow your own flowers. To be able to grow the flowers and foliages in the colors and shapes that you enjoy working with most is to add another dimension to your flower arranging. It is important to remember, however, that it is a shock to the cell formation of any plant material to be cut, and it is therefore important to treat the flowers with care and to condition them well them before attempting to use them in an arrangement.

As flowers lose moisture on sunny days it is advisable to avoid picking at mid-day or the afternoon; the best time to

pick is in the early evening when the sap is high, enabling you to condition the flowers overnight so that they are ready for arranging when you are both at your best in the morning. It sounds very romantic to trip around your garden with a rustic trug on your arm, but this is not the correct way to gather flowers. You should always carry a bucket of tepid water with you into the garden. As you select and gather your flowers, by making a slanted cut with a sharp knife or scissors, you can immediately place them in water, so avoiding airlocks and any chance of wilting. Think about the color and shape of the display you intend to make, and with that picture in mind pick only what you need and the length of stems that you require. Pick with care: don't leave holes in your flower

The flower arranger's essential props: lavendar (below); buddleia (right above); double poppy (far right above); delphinium (right below); and dahlia (far right below).

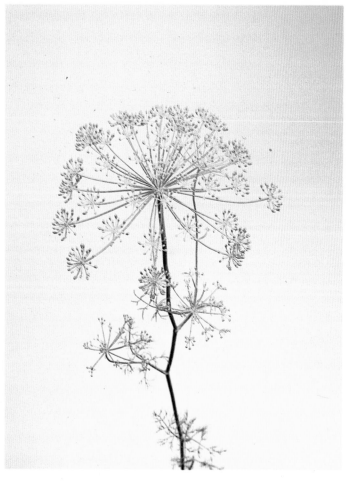

More flowers regularly used in arrangements: clockwise from top left, sweet pea, cornflower, scabious and fennel.

Alstroemeria (above and above right) and the glorious lily (right).

beds, but rather make it a thinning operation. When you are taking foliage always be careful to take branches from the rear of the shrub. If taking foliage from trees, do it in a way that will improve the shape and think in terms of pruning. After you have gathered flowers from your garden you should be able to challenge anyone to find the gaps.

The flowers to grow in your garden are very much a personal choice but I would recommend that all gardens should include Estrantia, Bells of Ireland, Carnations, Chinese Lanterns, Christmas Roses, Day Lilies, Eryngium, Forget-me-nots, Gladioli, Gypsophila, Hydrangea, Lady's Mantle, Marigolds, Peonies, Solomon's Seal, Stocks, Zinnia and a large choice of Roses. Among the most useful foliages for flower arrangers are Berberis, Ferns, Hosta, Mock Orange (Philadelphus), Pieris and Viburnum.

If you are not fortunate enough to have a garden and you are buying flowers, it is very important that you buy from a good florist who will have thoroughly conditioned the flowers before putting them on sale. You should always look critically before buying; there should be no sign of wilting or disease, the stems should feel fresh and the leaves should be crisp. If the flowers are in tight bud, such as tulips, make sure that there is some sign of color, otherwise they may not open. With a multi-headed flower such as freesia or delphinium, make sure that the lower flowers are just opening and certainly do not buy if there are signs that the lower florets have been removed. With chrysanthemums, make sure that the centered flowers are firm and show no signs of pollinating.

CONDITIONING

Conditioning of the flowers depends on the texture of the stem. Soft stemmed flowers just need to be cut off at an angle about one inch from the end with a sharp knife and then placed in clean tepid water. Always remove leaves from below water level to keep the water fresh. Medium hard stems such as roses should be cut at an angle and then split, scraping the last part of the bark away. Hard stems, for instance foliage, should have the bottom leaves removed and the stems gently crushed with a hammer. Large hollow stems like lilies and delphiniums need a little help to take water up. They should be trimmed with a sharp knife and tepid water should be poured into the stem. The stem is then plugged with a twist of absorbent cotton, which will continue to allow water to be absorbed and drawn up the stem, and the flower placed in deep tepid water.

There are many substances available now to prolong the life of flowers besides the many traditional methods, which include adding a spoonful of sugar, lemonade, an aspirin or charcoal to the water. The most important single requirement, however, is that the vase or container should be absolutely clean to start with, and topped up with clean water every day.

BLEEDING STEMS

Flowers such as euphorbias and poinsettias bleed a milky substance when cut and this must be sealed to prevent seepage. The sealing is done by holding the stem in a flame until the milky substance stops flowing. This substance is usually an irritant to many people, so you should wash your skin immediately.

These are some of the more formal and elegant flowers which serve the flower arranger so well: carnation (far left above); rose (near left above); spray chrysanthemum (far left below).

The dahlia (below left and below right) provides a rainbow of colors.

These delicate blooms barely look robust enough to form an arrangement: iris (above left); larkspur (above); orchid (left).

Michaelmas daisies (or New York daisies) combined with golden gerbera and alstroemeria (below), a detail of the arrangement on page 82/3.

27

Love-in-a-mist (left) features in several of the arrangements shown here, while the close-up below shows a detail of the arrangement on page 104, with antirrhinums, pot begonias and pot ferns.

African daisy (right above); sunflower (far right above); cornflower (right below); and Japanese anemone (far right below).

INTERIORS

Flowers add life to a room; they can be used to add warmth and serenity, or to give a focal point and distract the eye from a dull corner, or to complement a feature of furniture. Unlike the Victorian ladies, who scattered flowers all around the room bearing no relationship to any of the other objects in the room, today's flower arranger will consider with care the relationship of the arrangement to the setting in which it is to be placed. You should take into account the position and the scale and size of the arrangement, and the form and textures of the various objects close to the arrangement.

A hall can take a large arrangement; it should be warm and welcoming and a dominant shape that might serve as a good conversation starter. In the hall arrangement pictured (right), the miniature gladioli are protected and huddled into a formation of deliciously warm, soft love-lies-bleeding and should give any visitor a warm glow as they enter the hall.

Kitchen arrangements should be casual and easy on the eye. Flowers can be arranged in jugs or cups or pottery dishes and placed on shelves or mounted on the wall, while sweet-smelling herbs are ideal for making kitchen swags and wreaths. As the kitchen is a busy place, arrangements must be unobtrusive; the picture (below) demonstrates what I call an 'apple pie arrangement'. The mixed flowers are in a nice kitcheny bowl and have been inserted into dome-shaped florist's foam, so that even if the arrangement is knocked over in a busy kitchen the flowers will be steady and no water will leak from the arrangement, which is ideal for a kitchen table.

Flowers in an office or study should be thought-provoking and attract some critical attention. Flowers for the dining room are usually centered on a table and become most important when you are entertaining. A long thin boat-shape usually suits well for a dinner party. The height is of some importance; the diners need to be able to

It is worth waiting for the right time of year to use a pretty piece of china; as soon as the feverfew appears, this dish (left) comes out to be displayed to full advantage. It has been filled with dome-shaped florist's foam and the flowers have been cut short and positioned in groups to give an apple pie shape.
Plant materials: *Clove Spray Carnations, Feverfew, Yellow Stonecrop.*

The radiant soft trails of Love-Lies-Bleeding cascade down over this elegant black vase (right) with its cloisonné flowers, which confirm the color relationship between the soft tails of the Love-Lies-Bleeding and the vertical stems of the miniature gladioli rising out from the center.
Plant materials: *Love-Lies-Bleeding, miniature Gladioli.*

see one another over the arrangement. Candelabras can be very pretty above a dining table with the arrangements placed just under the candles. Flat tables and glass tables cannot take a fluffy cottage style arrangement. The flowers (overleaf) have been arranged in glass tumblers and in the center tumbler we have placed a white candle. The clear-cut lines of the lilies, daisies and ruscus foliage would work well in the setting of a modern table.

A flower arranger's creative skills can reach their full potential in a living room or sitting room, where the scope for different settings for flower arrangements will be manifold. The flowers arranged left have a soft outline, using bells of Ireland and lady's mantle, but also a very dominant center of lilies, which will make a good focal point in a sitting room. The *Pot-et-Fleurs* illustrated on page 104 would make a perfect arrangement for a fireplace during the summer months. The foliage and flowering plants could last the whole summer, while the small vase that is placed among the pot plants – and in this case has antirrhinum (snapdragons) arranged in it – can be readily

An exquisite summer table arrangement (previous pages) combines fruit and flowers to give a fresh outdoor feeling.
Plant materials: *Buddleia fallowiana, Fennel flowers, Gypsophila 'Baby's Breath', Alpine strawberries flowers and leaves.*

This beautiful, tied hostess bunch (left) has been slipped into a tall heavy vase, and the edges have been softened by adding a few sprays of lady's mantle from the garden.
Plant materials: *Blue Larkspur, Bells of Ireland, Yellow Spray 'Spider' Chrysanthemums, Lilium Mid-Century Hybrid 'Mont Blanc', Verbena.*

The leaf design on this classic-shaped pottery vase (right) harmonizes with the foliage of the striking orange lilies. By using lilies only in this arrangement, the single color is preserved and the opening stages of the flower formation can be appreciated.
Plant materials: *Lilium Mid-Century Hybrid 'Enchantment'.*

These green glass tumblers were the inspiration for a yellow and green design to run down the center of a table. The yellow lilies are interspersed with white spray daisy chrysanthemums, while dark green ruscus foliage is intertwined around the tumblers.
Plant materials: *Lilies, Spray Daisy Chrysanthemums, Ruscus foliage.*

The blues of Love-in-a-Mist are echoed in the color of the rounded mottled bowl, which in turn is balanced by this tight cone-shaped flower arrangement (overleaf left).
Plant materials: *Spiraea, Love-in-a-Mist, Honeysuckle, red leaves of Heuchera Palace Purple.*

This simple arrangement of cool-toned flowers (overleaf right) fills a niche in a bathroom.
Plant materials: *Poppies, Lavender.*

changed to give a continual abundance of color, showing how functional items like fireplaces can be complemented by the arrangement placed in them.

The curving stems of buddleia and the beautifully shaped marguerites on page 14 have been arranged on a pin holder in a flat dish. This would be shown to best advantage placed on a low coffee table, where it can be viewed from above. If flowers are to be placed in the center of the sitting room, where they will be viewed from all sides, an all-round flower decoration must be designed, as on pages 115 and 132. If, however, the arrangement is to go flat against a wall and to last for some time, an ideal arrangement would be that on page 107 which is a fan-shaped arrangement of mixed flowers.

Cloakrooms and restrooms demand scented but unobtrusive flower arrangements; the little rock roses arranged in the rose jug with the bouvardia (page 42) would be a perfect arrangement. Flowers for the bedroom should again be small and unobtrusive, and you need to take care that they cannot be knocked over in the dark. In a bathroom it is a nice idea to use glass containers, to echo the modern atmosphere of most bathrooms and so that the water and the naked stems of the plant material can be seen. The modern and meaningful arrangement (right) is intended to suggest that one vertical person showering uses just one tenth of the water that a horizontal person uses for a bath. Food for thought for the environmentally aware in the bathroom.

The design on the green jug (left) has been carefully worked into the arrangement by positioning the pink rambler rose to follow the line of the roses on the jug. This pretty arrangement is lightened by a mass of white bouvardia pouring out of the lip side of the jug. Plant materials: *Single Pink Rambling Roses, White Bouvardia.*

The rich color of these sumptuous lilies constrasts effectively with the dark russet foliage to make an informal arrangement that will grace any living room. Plant materials: *Lilium hybrid, Copper Beech foliage.*

A GUIDE TO FLOWER ARRANGING TECHNIQUES

WIRING

Wiring fresh flowers is rather frowned upon, but there are occasions when a wire can support a heavy flower head which might otherwise break; for example, a stub wire can be pushed up through the stem of a hyacinth to support the weight of the head. Flowers that have to be carried or worn are also usually wired so that they hold the shape of the design. This has the further advantage of reducing the weight of the arrangement. Wired flower techniques are also widely used in dried flower work.

Wire Stem

To make a wire stem for a rose, for use in a bouquet, cut the existing stem 1-inch (2.5cm) below the calyx. Push a 12 inch (30cm) 22-gauge wire through the calyx, extending to about one inch the other side, and bend down the wires, pinching one against the calyx and leaving the other to make a single wire leg. Conceal the wire by covering the calyx and the wire with gutta or stem tape.

Mounting Wires

Attaching wires to flowers allows them to be secured to a base. Bind a wire around a stem, leaving two 3-inch (7.5cm) wire 'legs' to be used for inserting. Lightweight flowers which are to be inserted into foam can be wired with reel wire. Plant material to be mounted into moss bases requires black stub wires with, optionally, one or two legs.

Taping

To conceal the wire holding the wired flower, place the gutta-percha or stem tape behind the calyx at a 45° angle. Tuck in the end and then twist the wire and continue twisting while holding the gutta taut, allowing it to creep down and cover the wire.

Bunching

This involves gathering together a selection of flowers, shortening the stems, and then binding them with black reel wire, leaving two 3-inch (7.5cm) wire legs to be mounted into foam, or cover with stem tape if they are to be used for bouquets and garlands.

Wiring Cones

Push one end of a 12-inch (30 cm) 20-gauge wire between the lowest scales of the cone, leaving about 1½ inch (4cm) of the short end protruding. Tightly wind the wire around and through the cone scales to meet the short end. Twist together to secure the cone, trim the short end flush, and then bend the wire under the base. Use stem tape or gutta to conceal the wire.

Pinning

This is the best way to attach stemless plant material to a base such as moss or foam. Cut black wires into 3½-inch (9 cm) lengths and bend them in half to form a two pronged 'pin', which you can then use to secure plant material such as lichen or flower heads to the base of foam or moss.

VARNISHING

Gourds and some seed cases can be treated with a layer of artist's clear gloss varnish from a spray can (available from art materials suppliers). A light spray with matt varnish will seal in some grass seeds, and can be used to stop other fragile items from shattering.

To preserve gourds, pierce both ends with a knitting needle or skewer and leave them in a warm place to dry. When the gourd is fully dry, the seeds can be heard rattling inside. Mount the dried gourd to hold it steady and spray one end. When it is dry, reverse it and spray the other end.

SPRAYING

Gold and silver colored spray paints can be used to change the appearance of cones, seedheads, etc. It is important that this is done in the open on a still day. For best results, mounted items can be inserted into a foam block, loose items placed on the floor of a large open cardboard carton. It is advisable to wear disposable plastic gloves to protect your hands from the spray. Shake the can well to get an even blend of color and spray the material liberally. When it is dry, turn it over and spray again, then leave to dry thoroughly.

BLEACHING

Grasses, branches and seedheads can be bleached by leaving them in a bowl of domestic bleach overnight. They must then be rinsed thoroughly and hung up to dry, heads down.

A GUIDE TO FLOWER DECORATION

MAKING A WREATH OR GARLAND

When is a garland not a wreath? If the ends of a garland are joined together, then it becomes a wreath, a word that has an unhappy connection with funerals for many people, probably because the Victorians, with their preoccupation with death, introduced a fashion for floral tributes in the shape of wreaths. Wreaths in previous ages were used at celebrations. Wreath headdresses made from olive and laurel leaves were awarded by the Greeks at the early Olympics. Julius Caesar was crowned with a laurel wreath, and in later centuries the bejeweled crowns worn by royalty took their name from the latin *corona*, a circlet for the head. This is why I have suggested a flower head-dress (see page 54) as the crowning glory on a wedding day.

You can purchase ready-made foam plastic wreath bases but these do not support heavy material well, and it is better to make your own moss wreath. Cut a piece of wire netting to the required length and about 12 inches (30cm) wide. You can work out the length by making a circle of string to the size you want, then opening it out and measuring it. Lay out the netting on a table. Make a mound of damp sphagnum moss all along the edge nearest to you. Now roll the wire netting away from you and over the moss to form a roll. To use it as a swag or garland, simply bend in the ends, but for a wreath bend the ends right around until they touch, then sew together with black reel wire.

BOWS

These can add a touch of celebration to a flower gift, and I think that the most beautiful bows are made from natural materials. The iridescent green color of the reverse side of iris leaves makes a particularly attractive decoration to be added to a silver container. Use the whole leaf for a flower arrangement, mounting it with a single stub wire leg. Push this well down in the damp foam so that the foliage can take up moisture. Use the same method when working with gladiolus foliage.

Alternatively you can make artificial bows with water resistant ribbon purchased from your local florist. Take a length of ribbon and form a figure of eight, holding the center between thumb and forefinger; with the same ribbon make another figure of eight, and join them at the center. Bind them together tightly with silver stub wire, leaving two mounting legs. If you find making bows difficult, you can instead mount single loops and insert several of these together, so imitating a fulsome bow.

This charming bow (right) made of satin ribbon shaped into two figures of eight and joined at the center will add the finishing touch to a presentation bouquet.

A GUIDE TO FLOWER ARRANGING MATERIALS

Most kitchens have several cookbooks and drawers and shelves full of cooking utensils, aids and accessories, but probably only one or two flower arranging books, if any, with no other accessories. There may be, at the bottom of a drawer, those nice pebbles picked up on the beach last summer; on a shelf that fascinating gourd that Uncle grew; and by the fire that twisted piece of wood you found on the heath. If you are new to the art of flower arranging, now is the time to gather all these useful items together, give them a new home (with room for expansion), and label them 'Flower Arranging Materials'. You may have only a few items now, and some vases, so here is a list of some of the materials used in the arrangements in this book, which will soon become a must when the flower arranging bug bites!

NATURAL MATERIALS

Bun or carpet moss This is used to cover soil and give a good finish to an arrangement of flowers. A quick gift can be made by dressing up a bowl of flowering bulbs with carefully positioned bun moss.

Cones Try to make a collection including cedar cones, Scots pine, larch and sugar pine. Some of them you will be able to pick up under the various trees in the winter. They should be washed or brushed clean and dried in a warm place. Cones can also be bought from your florist or from a specialist shop.

Driftwood A holiday must is a walk on the beach at low tide to search for interestingly shaped driftwood. Alternatively, if you find an interesting fallen branch in the woods, bring it home, scrub it clean and bleach it. Driftwood is also sold by specialist and florist shops. The term is also used to include cork bark and similar materials.

Fruits This includes berries, nuts and vegetables as well as the more usual apples and oranges.

Fungus Sponge fungus and golden mushrooms have exciting shapes and textures, invaluable for flower arrangements. You can dry fungus yourself, spread out on newspaper at the bottom of a warm cupboard, but a very wide range is available at specialist and some florist shops.

Gourds You can buy packets of mixed seeds and grow these yourself. Once again, however, a good variety is available at specialist shops.

Driftwood and cork (left) are both useful props for the keen flower arranger, and should be collected whenever the occasion arises. When using driftwood or fallen branches, always cut out any part that is soft, as it will rot; discard the whole branch if too much is affected.

Containers (right) can come in all shapes and sizes; you should gradually build up a good collection.

Lichen For flower arranging this usually means reindeer moss, gathered inside the Arctic Circle and dyed in many colours. It is useful for covering dry foam and the darker colors can be used to give depth to arrangements.

Lotus seed heads An exotic addition to any collection.

Rocks, stones and pebbles Flowers look their most natural when displayed against rocks or stones. These are also useful for disguising florist's mechanics.

Twisted or tortured willow This is an invaluable bare branch; just a small stem, five flowers, a pin holder and some pebbles are all you need to make a stunning display. Spray it with silver for a Christmas display.

ARTIFICIAL MATERIALS

Containers You can use anything that can be made to hold water, so the world is your oyster. Useful items from your home include boxes, miniature chests, letter racks, teapots and disguised jam and coffee jars. You will need to build up a good selection of Vases, varying in size, shape and circumference, and while you will always want to buy that special one you crave, it need not always be expensive. At carboot and jumble sales you can often find an old vase that has a good shape but an awful color or pattern, or a small amount of damage that can be repaired. Scrub it well, and when perfectly dry spray it with a can of matt paint to the color you require. Containers that are too large can have a smaller one placed inside them.

Glass nuggets These, available at good florist and specialist shops, are made in a wide range of colors and are useful for hiding florist's mechanics. They also work as a decorative support material (see page 61). A collection of pebbles and shells can be used in a similar way to show off their color and textures once submerged in water.

Paper ribbons These have the perfect texture to accompany and dress up dried flowers and make them into beautiful gifts.

Glass nuggets (right) come in many colors and are an invaluable flower arranging aid, whether for disguising the mechanics or enhancing the colors of an arrangement.

Paper ribbon (below) is usually sold twisted in rope form and needs to be unwound before being made up into bows.

A GUIDE TO FLOWER ARRANGING MECHANICS

Florist's mechanics is the term applied to any material used to hold or support both fresh and dried flowers in order to create arrangements.

ADHESIVE CLAY TAPE

Comes in a roll protected by a paper backing. It will stick firmly to glass, china, etc., and can be later removed without damage to the china. It will also stick to wood or fabric but is very difficult to remove from this, as it embeds itself in the grain.

DRI-HARD

A soft clay that dries hard in a few hours and can be used as a base for all types of dried flower arrangements.

'STAYSOFT'

Trade name for a type of reusable florist's plasticene which can hold a small display of dried flower stems.

FLORIST'S FOAM

First introduced in the 1950s, foam quickly became a favorite tool for holding floral arrangements and has advantages over wire mesh, particularly when used in difficult positions.

Green foam is available in blocks and is intended for fresh flowers and must be well soaked in warm water for four minutes. Do not force it under the water (which will cause air bubbles to remain in the block), but let it soak up water, unassisted, Green foam can be used with most flowers and foliage except soft stemmed and very heavily stemmed flowers, which are best supported by chicken wire. It must not be allowed to dry out in use. In many cases it can be re-used, if in the meantime it has been kept soaked in a watertight plastic bag. To re-use green foam, take the foam out of the bag, re-soak it in fresh water, and turn it over so that what was the bottom now becomes the top.

Brown foam is available in cylinders, cones, ovals and balls as well as in blocks for easy use in variously shaped containers. It is a firmer substance than the green, and is used with dried and silk flowers. It will not absorb water and can be easily cut with a large sharp kitchen or carving knife. It is very lightweight and must be securely fixed into its container. The container itself may need to be weighted if it is supporting a large display, to prevent it overbalancing.

This 'wet type' florist's foam block (right) is held down in the container with florist's securing tape.

Plastic pinholders, secured with adhesive tape, are pushed into a wet type foam black (left).

Traditional florist's scissors (below) are used for cutting stems and wires, while lightweight ones (bottom) are best for trimming flowers and foliage and cutting ribbon.

FLORIST'S SCISSORS

These are a must for cutting through hard stems and wires, and for all general heavy work. Wire cutters are a useful extra for cutting thick wires, white lightweight florist's scissors are best for trimming flowers and cutting ribbon.

PIN HOLDER

These are lead weights inset with a pattern of steel pins to hold and support stems. They can be used on their own in shallow containers to support plant stems, or combined with wire mesh in deep containers, which may necessitate more support. Stems can be impaled on the pins or held at an angle between them.

PLASTIC PIN HOLDERS OR CANDLE SPIKES

These are embedded in foam blocks, which are then fixed to their container with adhesive clay tape.

QUICK-DRYING GLUE

This is useful for attaching false stems to dried flower heads. Alternatives are a hot glue gun or a quick-drying tube glue, but you should handle these with caution and take care to use only the minimum. The glue will also be useful for attaching dried flowers and bows to baskets.

Stem tape (right) is used to disguise wired stems and comes in various colors. Gutta-percha is the original florist's material, made from a natural tree gum similar to rubber, while stem tape is man-made.

Wire cutters (below) can be used for cutting heavy wire, to preserve your florist's scissors.

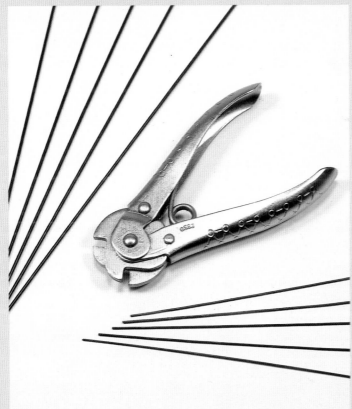

STEM TAPE and GUTTA-PERCHA

These are thin, colored tapes used to wind around wired stems to conceal the mechanics. As it is stretched it sticks to itself. Available in white, green and brown.

WIRE

This is not used a great deal for fresh flower work, with the exception of corsage and bouquet work. Wire also allows a great deal of weight, in the form of unwanted stems, to be removed from the finished work. Wires are now used a great deal more in dried flower work. Varieties include black stub wire for making false stems and supporting limp ones – medium gauge is the most useful ; silver and black wire for mounting; silver and black reel wire for bunching and binding.

WIRE MESH NETTING

Usually referred to as chicken wire, this is one of the most useful of the florist's tools. Buy it by the meter from a hardware store or ironmonger. 2-inch (5cm) mesh is best, as it crumples very easily, is not too rigid to be 'molded', and is cheaper than smaller mesh sizes.

To use wire mesh measure out a length that is twice the diameter of the container and cut it with a pair of florist's scissors. Crumple it evenly to a size that will fit into the container and then use the points of the scissors to lift and move it about to space it evenly. Secure the mesh to the container by tying in with string, reel wire or florist's fixing tape, according to the type of container you are using.

SECURING TAPE

This is a semi-waterproof self-adhesive fixing tape used to secure foam blocks or wire netting to a container.

STEM STRIPPERS

These are used for clearing stem ends of foliage.

WEDDINGS

A wedding day is one of the most important occasions in anyone's life, and it is a day when the bride's wishes are paramount. When choosing and arranging flowers for a wedding, you should give every consideration to the bride's coloring, the style of her gown, and the style and coloring of her bridesmaids. The toning of all the flowers should be in keeping with her choice of colors for her big day. The practice of carrying flowers for a wedding dates back at least to the sixteenth century, and much earlier still the Romans and the Greeks wore garlands in their hair at their ceremonies. The Greeks have regarded orange blossom as a sign of fertility for hundreds of years, and in many European countries rosemary, for remembrance and also for fertility, is added to a bride's flowers.

The choice of flowers for a bride is very variable and depends very much on the style of her dress. The country bride might well choose to carry an informal posy of mixed country flowers, below as shown. With its center of yellow roses, daisies and cornflowers and lady's mantle, this posy, with a lovely garland for the bride's head, will together add up to a vision of a traditional country wedding.

This traditional Victorian posy (left) would be perfect for a country bride to carry on her wedding day. The tightly bunched bright summer flowers with their matching headdress would look striking against a white or ivory wedding dress.
Plant materials: *Yellow Roses, Blue Cornflowers, Marguerites, Lady's Mantle, Lady's Mantle foliage.*

The high point for celebratory flowers is a wedding day. Here the foliage is positioned to frame the flowers (right) so that they will stand out from the dress in the photographs to be taken on the day. The bouquet includes heather for luck, rosemary for remembrance and myrtle for true love, from which the bride could strike cuttings.
Plant materials: *Roses, Pinks, Heather, Rosemary, Myrtle, Ivy, Fern, Alpine Alchemilla Mollis foliage.*

The bouquet featured above and in the step by step arrangements on pages 56-57 is suitable for a bride who wishes to tone her flowers in with the peach and coral material of the bridesmaids' dresses. The flowers are shown off by using plenty of ivy and fern foliage; included in the bride's bouquet is white heather for luck, rosemary for tradition, and myrtle to signify love. The same bride could choose to carry a lasting bouquet of dried flowers and the picture on page 140 illustrates a bouquet of dried peonies, roses and *Eucalyptus robusta*.

Step by step instructions

1. Cut foliage into small pieces and wire with a 22-gauge wire, Wire heavy flowers with 18-gauge wire.

2. Take small spray roses and wire them with silver wires. Cover the wires with tape and group these together with a 22-gauge wire.

3. Cover all wires with stem tape.

4. Starting with heather and the small sprays of flowers, wire the stems together using reel wire. Continue to bind in the foliage and flowers and make a triangular shape, moving the wire down to make a firm handle. When this is about 9 inches long, bind firmly in the same position while building up height for the center of the bouquet. Now bend the flowers at right angles to the stem to form a handle, add the remainder of the flowers to form the top of the bouquet, and continue to bind in the same position. Trim the bouquet and cover in stem tape. Then cover the handle with white ribbon and add a bow to the back of the bouquet.

The spray below is made up of eucalyptus leaves and white tuberose, and would be a very suitable shoulder spray for the mother of the bride. Alternatively, the same spray could be placed on top of a white bible or prayer book with a ribbon added, and would then be ideal for the bride to carry.

If the bride is wearing an elegant dress of plain white satin, then a simple and restrained bouquet of lilies, tied into a bunch with a plain satin ribbon, would look most suitable on her arm. Brocade requires textured flowers such as stephanotis and orchids, while lace looks best with softer-textured blooms, such as lily-of-the-valley, roses,

The finely carved appearance of the waxen and fragrant tuberose has a lustrous richness which makes it a perfect flower for a corsage, while the small feathery leaves of eucalyptus foliage make an excellent background. This corsage could also be used as a spray for a bride on a bible or prayer book.

Plant materials: *Tuberose, Eucalyptus.*

Step by step instructions

1. Push a silver stub wire up into the flower. Take another silver wire, push it through the base of the stem and twist it to the original wire.

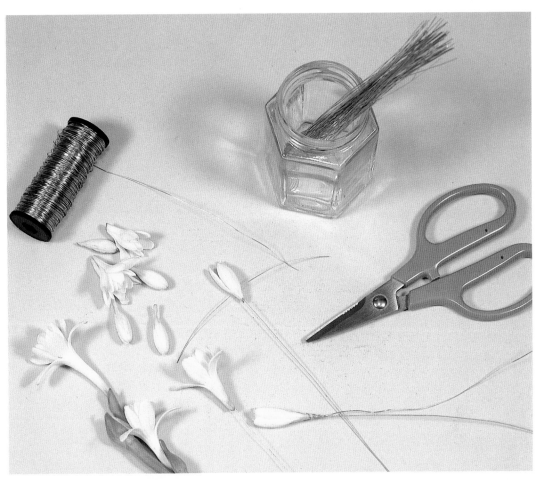

2. Break the eucalyptus into small sprays and twist a wire round the stem.

3. Using stem tape, carefully cover the base of the flowers and foliage and the wires with the tape. Starting with a piece of foliage and the smallest bud of tuberose, carefully bind the stems together, using silver wire, and cover with tape. Add more flowers and foliage to build up a triangular shape, using the most open tuberose at the base of the triangle. At this point bind in the remaining buds and foliage, bend backward to make a return end. Trim wires, bind together with silver wire and cover with stem tape.

4. Wire together small bunches of bleached broom bloom and use these to fill in the gaps in the basket.

This bridal bouquet (far right) is in a delightfully asymmetrical style. The autumnal colors of the Boston Vine leaves form a background to the flowers, so that they stand out against the bride's dress.

Plant materials: *Autumn leaves of Boston Vine, leaves of Leucothoe fontanesiana 'Rainbow', Carnation, Lily-of-the-valley, gold-rayed Lily Lillium auratum, Rose.*

Flower decorated pew ends make a warm welcome for the bride as she walks to the altar. The flowers (left) are arranged on a solid block of soaked florist's foam; wires are attached to this that can hang from the pew end, while plastic film protects the back. The soft foliage outline is strengthened by the spiky flowers, which build up to a focal point of pink open gladioli and lilies.

Plant materials: Cotoneaster foliage, Clematis foliage, White Larkspur, Pink Gladioli, Lilium Mid-Century Hybrid 'Montreux', Gypsophila.

gypsophila and freesia. If the bride is wearing pure white and wishes to carry white flowers, her bouquet needs a good variety of green foliage to set off the flowers, or they will disappear into her dress in the photographs. Very often a bride will choose flowers that tone with the colors of her bridesmaids' dresses. If her own dress is off-white or an ivory color, care should be taken in using white flowers, and it is best to persuade her to opt for cream and peach shades, which look beautiful on ivory silk.

Maids of honor may carry a formal bouquet but this should be smaller than the bride's, usually in deeper toning flowers, while small bridesmaids look delightfully attractive with a little posy, a ball of flowers on a ribbon, or even a hoop with flowers arranged on it. The fashion is back to wearing garlands in the hair rather than on a more formal headpiece, which looks wonderfully attractive and romantic; these flowers should match the flowers in the bouquet. All flowers to be carried at a wedding should be prepared only a few hours before the ceremony, otherwise they will wilt.

The groom may wear a flower to match the bride's bouquet or a white carnation in his buttonhole – do make sure that he has a buttonhole in his jacket. Ushers usually wear a red carnation or a flower that matches the bridesmaids' colors.

In the case of a church or synagogue wedding or other religious ceremony, it is important to organize the flowers to co-ordinate with the needs of the clergy. Visit the church or synagogue to check how the daylight will fall at the time of the wedding and to make sure that the colors of the altar cloth or hangings will not clash with the bride's color scheme. As most flower arrangements in the church will be seen from some distance away, they need to be large massed arrangements with bold outlines. Most churches are dimly lit and light-colored flowers will stand out well, but you must be wary of placing flowers on windows in a church as the light will make it very difficult to see them. In some cases light can enhance a lacey plant, like Queen Anne's lace or ornamental grasses, but otherwise it is best to use solid outlines and certainly do not place flowers in front of stained glass windows. In a modern church it is best to do a modern arrangement rather than a traditional one, which will be more in keeping with the clear-cut lines of a modern church.

Pew-end arrangements can be very effective arranged on a foam base, using flowers to tone with the bride's bouquet and ribbons to trail romantically to the ground. These can be placed on every or alternate pew ends, or a very large arrangement can be placed at the end of the top pew only, as illustrated left.

If a wedding budget is limited it is very important to have at least one large pedestal arrangement near the place in the church where the couple exchange their vows. Some people find a pedestal arrangement a daunting thing

Step by step instructions for the pedestal arrangement on page 67

1. Select a shallow container and, using a sharp knife, shape blocks of soaped florist's foam to fill the front half of the container. Fill the back half of the container with a block that is two inches higher than the front.

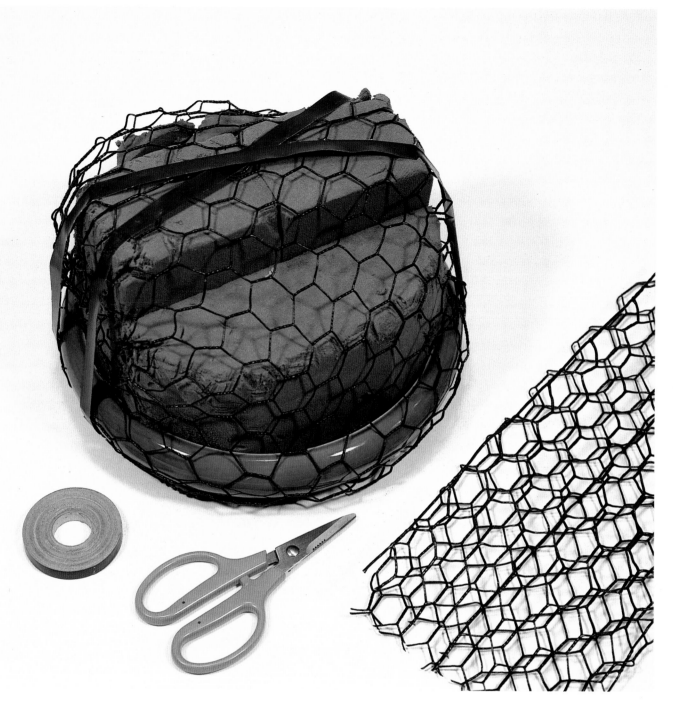

to tackle, but the step by step pictures (pages 63-67) showing how the arrangement is built up shows that the most important thing is to sort out the mechanics. Use plenty of foliage to give outline and shape, and then use bold flowers to give definition and authority to the arrangement. You do not necessarily need a lot of flowers, but they must be strong and bold in color.

With all the hustle and bustle of preparation for a wedding, it is very important for the bride to leave home feeling calm. Flowers in the hall of the bride's home should therefore be serene, and the monochrome elegance of the arrangement of stock and curling tortured willow (pages 68-69) is ideal.

2. Completely cover the foam and the edges of the container with wire netting. Secure this with florist's waterproof fixing tape. Place it on the pedestal and check that the mechanics are firm.

3. Position foliage to form a fan shape, sloping back slightly to give added depth. Form sides and front by positioning the foliage with the stems upwards.

4. Position all the gladioli stems, keeping the shaped defined by the foliage, and at the same time fill in with more foliage. Intersperse with the remaining flowers. If the back of this pedestal arrangement is to be on view, short stems of foliage must be positioned to cover the mechanics.

The formal fan shape of the finished arrangement is easily achieved by carefully placing the dominant stems of gladiolus. The substantial foundation of foliage used in this display allows the flowers to be used economically.

Plant materials: Gladioli, Roses, Scabius, Forsythia foliage, Quince foliage, Thistle leaves.

A grid of wire netting has been stretched across the neck of this lovely glass vase and secured with florist's tape. The soft curls of the twisted willow foliage complement the soft blossoms on the stems of white stock which follow their natural leanings when placed in the vase. The star-shaped flowers of tobacco plant (nicotiana) make a striking focal point among all these soft curves. Both flowers produce a delicious fragrance.
Plant materials: *Branches of Tortured Willow, White Stock, Tobacco Plant.*

A suitably rich arrangement for an engagement party.
Plant materials: *White and Red Roses, Gypsophila Baby's Breath.*

FLOWERS FOR THE RECEPTION

Be sure to place flowers where they can be seen. If a reception area is full of guests it is no use placing flowers at ground level, and it is important to get flowers high up on pedestals, mantelpieces and windowsills. If the reception is in a marquee, wonderful opportunities are afforded to display flowers among the billowing folds of canvas. The supporting poles of the marquee can be decorated with cascading garlands of flowers, left and as demonstrated in the step by step guide below and overleaf. Buffet tables can be ornamented with clusters and garlands of flowers, pedestals, pyramids and candelabras, mixtures of fruit and flowers also look very attractive and make an imaginative and extravagant arrangement.

This sumptuous wedding garland (far left) can be used to adorn the supporting poles of a marquee, twisted round banisters, or suspended from a ceiling.

Step by step instructions

1. Cut a block of florist's foam into eight pieces.

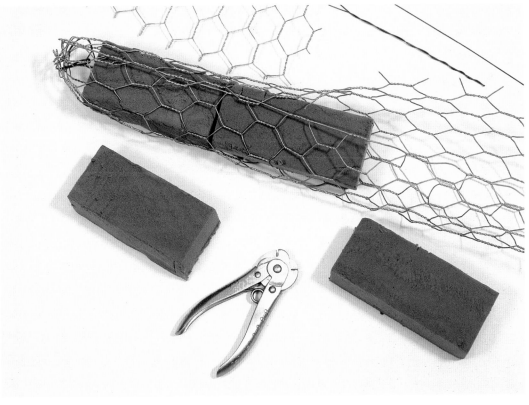

2. Cut a length of wire netting and bind it round the pieces of foam, making a wire hook at each end.

3. Using wire pins, cover the foam with foliage.

4. Cut flowers and foliage short and push large flowers into the foam. Wire small groups of mixed flowers together and intersperse them between the large flowers. Continue along the full length of the garland and then attach the hook wire to the top of the pole and twist the garland round. Then carefully adjust it and add flowers as necessary to give a balanced display.

Crowning the wedding cake (right), roses and lily of the valley are displayed in a pyramid shape and then tipped over the edge of the top tier so that they cascade down to meet a circle of roses bursting from between the tiers of cake. A decorative arrangement of open roses and petals is placed around the cake to balance the composition.
Plant materials: *Lily of the Valley, White Roses, Pink Roses, Fern.*

THE WEDDING CAKE

Some of the most successful and memorable photographs of a wedding are often taken as the bride and groom cut the cake, as by this time they are relaxed and enjoying themselves. Some of the most beautiful flowers should therefore be placed on and around the wedding cake.

As the cutting of the cake for the photograph is usually just a token, the cake then being removed to be cut by the caterers, there is no practical reason why real flowers should not be used. They can be easily removed in the kitchen before the caterers slice the cake. Just as the flowers used in the bouquets will be out of water for a

minimum of six hours, so there is no reason why all the flowers decorating the cake should be in water. They should be given a long drink first, and the flowers on top of the cake can be arranged in a piece of florist's foam, the base of which has been covered in polythene. The flowers used between the cake layers should be clean, dry and un-perfumed. They should be tucked between the layers to give the appearance of spilling over, tumbling and cascad-ing onto the table. A selection of open flowers and petals should be scattered around the base of the cake, leaving a space for the bride's bouquet to be put into position for when the photographs are taken.

73

CELEBRATIONS

Whether an anniversary, a personal gift or a seasonal celebration, the mood of the moment can always be captured in flowers.

NEW HOME

One of the nicest ways to celebrate someone moving to a new home is to send them flowers, but you must allow for the fact this is a very busy time for people. They will not be able to arrange flowers or even spend much time looking at them over the few days of unpacking boxes, etc. The scented garland depicted on page 78 makes a beautiful and trouble-free gift. This herbal garland could be featured anywhere in the house, and will give a lovely scent to any room. It will last for weeks and can eventually be placed in the kitchen, where the herbs can actually be cut off and used as they dry. Another suitable gift would again be a *pot et fleurs* (page 104, 20), and again this takes little work as the flowers can just be put in position. The flowers mixed in with the plants would only last a matter of days, but by then the recipient would have time to replace just a few flowers or even simply enjoy the plants in the bowl.

These long-stemmed red roses (below) have been simply arranged and tied into a beautiful presentation bunch. The recipient can quickly cut and split the ends and then slip them into an upright vase for an instant arrangement. St Valentine was martyred in Rome as long ago as 269. Plant materials: Long-stemmed Red Roses 'Baccara'.

The fragrant sweet pea originated in Sicily and was first cultivated in 1698. These sweetly perfumed, variously shaded flowers (right) slip naturally into this square glass container. They are at their best when they match the informality of the dish and always create a charming fragrant effect. Plant materials: Mixed Sweet Peas, Maidenhair foliage.

VALENTINE

Traditionally Valentine's Day is associated with the beautiful red rose of love. Roses on their own, beautifully arranged into a hostess bunch and decorated with a sumptuous bow (left), mean that the recipient only has to place these in a vase to enjoy the glorious message of love. Alternatively, if a lasting gift is required, then a pleasing basket can be made up as shown on page 125, using dried red roses and dried gypsophila, the tiny one called Baby's Breath.

MOTHER'S DAY

Mother's Day is a traditional time for giving flowers. One of the most beautifully scented flowers for this purpose is the sweet pea, which is often known as the diamond of flowers. The beautiful hues and shades of the sweet pea can quickly be gathered into a small posy surrounded by delicate sprays of maidenhair fern (above). If this is presented wrapped in cellophane and decorated with a small bow, it can be dropped into a small container with disturbing the arrangement.

The mixed herbs used in this pretty garland (above) will give a heavenly aromatic perfume to the house. A mossed wreath has been used for a base, while clumps of herbs have been wired together and mounted into the moss to build up a circular shape. The wreath will dry naturally and still look pretty, while the dried herbs can gradually be cut off and used for culinary purposes.
Plant materials: *Thyme, Sage, Southernwood, Basil, Oregano, Poppy seedheads.*

78

Here is a superb garland which celebrates a wedding or a christening, or decorates a door at Christmas.
Plant materials: *Norway*

Spruce, Scots Pine, Cupressus, Ivy, Holly, Box, dried Canary Grass, Gypsophila, Poppy Seedheads covered in glitter.

79

BIRTHDAY

How uplifting on your birthday morning, amongst all the bowed boxes and wrapped gifts, to receive a basket of flowers that breathes garden. We have decorated a charming basket below by using garden asters and have added texture to this by including a branch of blackthorn bearing sloe berries, which have a beautiful bloom on them. As a concession to a birthday gift we have added a pretty bow.

Asters are a singularly beautiful flower whose Latin name translates as 'Lovely wreath of ray flowers from China'; the seed from China was first cultivated in France in 1730. This arrangement allows the observer to view the sheer beauty of the petal formation of these asters, while a sharp contrast of texture is supplied by the bunch of sloe berries cascading over the basket. Cut short and closely massed into the basket, the shape of each flower is still preserved and provides the main interest for the arrangement. Ribbon bows are added to complete this gift basket.

Plant materials: *Mixed Asters.*

In this Easter design the focal position of the eggs emphasizes the space above in relationship to the sweep of the rising line of iris and carnations.
Plant materials: *Iris, Carnations, Spray Carnations, Daisies, Chinese foliage.*

EASTER

Easter is one of the most important festivals in the Christian calendar, and an ideal opportunity to use flowers for decorating the home or workplace. The traditional choice is white lilies in churches, and homes decorated with spring flowers and Easter eggs. We have designed an arrangement which combines the traditional spring iris with a sharp yellow carnation, and also incorporating some white hens' eggs nestling at the foot of the arrangement to give a fresh spring feeling.

81

GOLDEN ANNIVERSARY

As more of us live into our gracious eighties and nineties, silver, golden, ruby and diamond wedding anniversaries are becoming more common. These are a wonderful occasion for a family celebration, an opportunity to bring together far-flung relations who otherwise probably only meet at weddings and funerals.

Fifty glorious years together is a marvelous occasion to celebrate with flowers, and naturally one should use as many golden flowers as possible. Here we have used golden gerbera and alstroemaria, arranged in a bold outline and using the less significant pale shades of Michaelmas daisy (New York daisy) and golden rod (*solidaster luteus*) to provide the structure and show off these beautiful golden flowers in an arrangement which will last for some time.

*The lateral branches of the
Michaelmas daisies (aster or
New York daisies) are loosely
spaced in a formal fan shape and
provide a background for the
golden gerbera and alstroemeria,
which are centrally placed and
swing down over the earthy
tones of the terracotta container.*
Plant materials: *Michaelmas
Daisy, Gerbera, Alstroemeria.*

THANKSGIVING

For hundreds of years, and especially since the Pilgrim Fathers celebrated the first New England harvest, we have been giving thanks at harvest time for the ripening of our crops, and it is a time of year when all the flowers reflect the rich color of the harvest. If you are having a Thanksgiving party or Harvest Supper, this is an occasion for an arrangement depicting all these beautiful colors, fruits and vegetables. Here (overleaf) we have hollowed out a pumpkin and a marrow and have filled these with soaked florist's foam as a base in which to arrange the flowers. The shape of the cut top of the pumpkin was so delightful that we could not bear to discard it and so it has been used in the grouping as a candle holder. The arrangement has the rich glow of autumn and would look delightful for a Thanksgiving display.

CHRISTMAS

No matter what people's cultural background, 25 December seems to be time for decorating the home with garlands and lights, and dried and fresh foliage arrangements. In recent years artificial garlands have become so lifelike, and the use of dried flowers and various ribbons so widespread, that it is difficult to persuade people to make real flower and foliage garlands, which will not last very well over a long seasonal holiday in a centrally heated apartment. I therefore advocate that one special place in the home should be left for a really large, fresh fruit and foliage arrangement that will give the spirit of Christmas. We have used various bowls and wooden plinths, together with the mechanical aids of florist's foam and wire mesh, to build up a strong base on which to place our candles and to arrange fruit, red carnations, holly and ivy to give a glorious Christmas feel (right).

GRADUATION

Graduation is a time when many proud parents wish to celebrate but most youngsters feel rather embarrassed, and so parents must be very careful not to go over the top on this occasion. We have presented our arrangement (right) using glass nuggets to support the stems, and have chosen the clear-cut lines of white cyclamen and blue delphinium. The modern style of this arrangement should please and intrigue the new graduate.

This sumptuous Christmas display (left) will intrigue the observer and invites close scrutiny. Wooden columns covered with foam and wire netting support the candles of unequal height. The main column is covered with a seasonal mixture of foliage, fruit and flowers, which descends in a riot of rich textures and radiant colors.
Plant materials: *Holly, Pine, Ivy, Broom Bloom, Lauristinus, Carnations, Roses, Spray Carnation, Apples, Grapes, Cotoneaster, Rosehip, Spruce, Cupressus.*

This combination of traditional Christmas blooms makes a change from potted plants.
Plant materials: *Poinsettia, Variegated Holly, Dried Red Berries.*

The soft shapes of the autumn vegetables suggested the containers for this stunning display, suitable for a Thanksgiving Supper. The gourd marrows and pumpkin have been hollowed out to receive a colorful combination of flowers expressing the ripeness of autumn. The flowers have been positioned to follow the soft curves of the marrow. Berries and apples slip over the edge of the pumpkin to continue the design into the discarded top of the pumpkin, which is used to support the candles.
Plant materials: Chinese Lanterns, Lilies, Dahlias, Spray Chrysanthemums, Istroemeria, Rosehips, Apples, Pumpkin, Marrow/Squash gourds.

MODERN

This chapter features flowers which in some countries would be considered exotic, although in others very ordinary. Air freight is changing the availability of flowers and it is worthwhile when buying flowers to ask your florist where they were growing forty eight hours earlier. Some of these long-distance blooms are quite expensive to buy, but do remember that most of them have long-lasting properties. Bearing this is mind, the designs in this chapter are made using very few blooms. You may feel that your home can only cope with traditional designs, but I hope that you will be open-minded and still study the shapes and take an interest in the symbolic designs. We have included a few historical notes to help you take an interest in flowers you may not have used before.

Thus far we have concentrated on flowers for the traditional home, but many people live in a modern home or wish to arrange flowers for a modern office. Modern design gives the creative artist the opportunity to use some of the more unusual plant material found in nature in a very stimulating way. Most modern flower designs use minimal flowers and are therefore most economical. If you are accustomed to the more traditional arrangements we have illustrated so far, your eye will need time to adjust. These arrangements incorporate the prevailing space into every design; the designs are very fluid and are often dictated by the plant material used.

Unlike traditional flower arrangements, which usually use a massed abundance of flowers, a modern design will have a simplicity of line and will allow the designer to use his or her creative inspiration to fashion the living material into a portrayal of their own ideas.

CYBIDIUM ORCHID

The cybidium orchid is one of the most exotic and long-lasting orchids that can be grown at home. Each flower has a short individual stem growing from a long curved stalk. In its tropical habitat this plant grows on the bark of a tree, and for this reason we have given the orchid the protection of its natural environment and have featured this spray of orchids (overleaf) nestling in a curl of Portuguese tree bark.

STRELITZIA

Strelitzias are natives of South Africa and belong to the banana family, as their leaves reveal. The most generally known strelitzia is the Bird of Paradise, recognized by its striking blue and orange bird-like blossom. Its elegant beauty looks best when standing alone in a distinctive setting as shown on page 95. Strelitzia are long-lasting but they need manipulating; as each blossom fades it must be removed and the next blossom forced out of its boat-shaped covering. Our design uses two pieces of driftwood, five stems of bird's nest fern, and one strelitzia flower, to give a very modern picture. The bird's nest fern bursts at various levels from the driftwood to give ground cover to the symbolic bird on top of the tree.

EASTER LILY

The simplicity and exquisite beauty of the Easter lily is portrayed in so many paintings of the past. In using it for an arrangement (right), the waxy appearance and exquisite formation of each flower must be carefully displayed, allowing its full beauty to be appreciated. The purity of line should be emphasized by displaying the stems in glass.

DRIFTWOOD

Driftwood can always add an extra dimension to a flower design, and is one of the most useful materials that a flower designer can acquire. The exciting and dynamic shapes of the various twisted roots and tree branches that are washed up on a beach will quickly become the prized possession of any flower arranger. If you are not lucky enough to live near the seashore, country walks can often prove fruitful for finding nice twisted roots and branches. If they are soft or starting to rot, discard them immediately, but if they are firm and hard taken them home, scrub them well, cut out any soft parts, and allow them to dry. If you want a lighter color you can always soak them in a solution of diluted bleach and then dry them out. With the aid of glues, screws, driftwood clamps and plaster of paris, several pieces of driftwood can be combined to make exciting sculptural formations which will give an interesting rhythm, movement and texture as a base for your flower arrangements.

Artists have long used the lily as a symbol of purity. The waxen buds open to reveal the perfectly formed trumpet, whose glorious, pure, radiating outline fits so perfectly in the holy setting in which it is so often placed. The various stages of the opening flowers are advantageously expressed in this design. The stems are supported by the container of Swedish glass, and the green of the glass accentuates the whiteness of the lilies.
Plant materials: *Easter Lilies, Choisya foliage.*

In the nineteenth century hundreds of British orchid hunters went into the jungles of tropical Asia and brought out many varieties of orchids. This was the beginning of a new worldwide interest in the largest known family in the plant kingdom. There are now over 20,000 specimens, and many hybrids that have been cultivated by cross-breeding. Orchids are now cultivated in the United States, South Africa, Australia and New Zealand; they have long-lasting properties and can survive between three and five weeks. In this arrangement (below) we have used a small spray of cymbidium orchid, with its waxy flowers and strongly

shaped marked lip. The spray in its glass phial has been tucked into a sweep of Portuguese bark, taking it back to its natural environment. Curled leaves of false palm have been used for the background.
Plant materials: *Cymbidium 'Piedmont', False Palm leaves 'Cordyline Terminala'.*

Other exotic plants were brought to the western world for cultivation during the nineteenth century (right). Native species were also used, although unfamiliar to settlers and colonists.
Plant materials: *Pink Anthurium, Palmetto leaves.*

BELLS OF IRELAND

Generally admired for its shell-shaped sepals which protect the very insignificant flower, this stem originated in Syria. It is the striking green of the long stem that gives it is modern name, green being the Irish national color. Bells of Ireland have small heart-shaped leaves and must be defoliated when used as a cut flower, to help them drink. In the design (left) the dark foliage of the echinops or globe thistle surrounding the massed heads of the cerise-colored spiraea contrasts sharply with the strange shapes and curves of the bells of Ireland. This design demands a commanding position.

The studied placement of this exquisite strelitzia bloom (right) has been achieved by positioning the curly leaves of bird's nest fern in the base of two vertical pieces of driftwood. This creates the illusion of a jungle, with the Bird of Paradise strelitzia poised for flight.
Plant materials: Strelitzia Bird of Paradise, Bird's Nest Fern, driftwood.

ARTICHOKE

The artichoke is a magnificent plant to grow in a vegetable patch. The silvery-gray flower buds are not only a gastronomic delicacy but also a visual delight. Note the interesting formation of the scale-like bracts, which gradually open as the plant ripens to reveal a handsome thistle of purple hairs. At this stage it will dry well and keep its color. It is therefore a flower of multi-dimensional use, as food, and as fresh and dried decoration. We have chosen to illustrate it (right) with a design of textures. The textured ceramic dish is mounted with the soft petals of clove carnations, the prickly seed-heads of love-lies-bleeding and downy-textured plums, contrasting with the sharpness and angular formation of the globe artichokes. The deep maroon shades contrast with the green grays.

IKEBANA

This is the Japanese word meaning the arrangement of plant material; the Japanese use few flowers, and the simple line of their arrangements depends mainly on the use of branches and grasses. Modern Ikebana, though far removed from the original temple arrangements, requires many years of study and is still imbued with a spiritual significance, giving great peace of mind and a deep understanding of life to those who study it.

The current interest in Ikebana owes much to Ellen Gordon Allen, the wife of an American general who was posted to Japan after the Second World War. Having studied Ikebana while in Japan, she missed it on returning to America, and formed Ikebana International in 1955. The aims of this association were to stimulate and cultivate the continuous study and spread of Ikebana, and to develop and improve an understanding of Japanese people and hence foster a better understanding between all nationalities.

There are many schools of Ikebana. The most modern was founded in 1920 and is called Sogetsu School. It teaches *Nageire*, meaning 'throwong in of flowers', usually in an upright container. Another common form is *Moribana* meaning 'piling up of flowers' on a flat container. These two styles are most suited to the Western home. When studying Ikebana, you are taught how to take plant material and quietly study its natural flow and lines, to feel in harmony with the material and unhurriedly to form a pleasing arrangement in harmony with the container and the base. The study also includes an understanding of the symbolism perceived, for example, in the fall of a branch. But much of this symbolism must come from one's own self knowledge and a deep understanding of life.

Ikebana cannot be adequately illustrated by one picture.

The multi-textured plant material used in this arrangement (above) was inspired by the texture of the leaf-shaped dish. The hard tooth-shaped petals of the artichoke and the spiky prickles that encase the soft seed pod contrast with the dewy look of the plums and the soft formation of the carnation petals.
Plant materials: Artichoke, Clove Carnation Spray, Love-in-a-Mist seed pods, Plums.

This symbolic arrangement in the Ikebana style (right) suggests a sunflower refreshed by the summer rain.
Plant materials Sunflowers, bleached Branch.

Our illustration (right) shows a symbolic arrangement in the style of Ikebana, to demonstrate a sunflower bowing its head in summer as it is refreshed by the summer rain, represented by the bleached branches slanting down towards earth and falling into a pool of rain at the base of the container. The background suggests threatening clouds, while the frenzied pattern of the upright container gives the feeling of swirling winds.

ANTHURIUM

This means 'tail flower'; it has developed many other common names in recent years including flamingo plant, wax flower and oilcloth flower. It originates from the rain forests of Columbia, was first cultivated in France in 1876, and is one of the most dramatic and showy florist's flowers. The brilliant colors and waxen texture of the flat heart-shaped spathe (pair of bracts) forms a base for the true flower, the spadix (tail) of densely packed tiny blossoms. It is a robust flower and will last about a month.

A low wooded bowl is used to advantage to display specimen blossoms.
Plant materials: *Yellow Lilies, Fig Foliage.*

98

ERYNGIUM PLANUM

These splendid steely clusters of thistles, also known as sea holly, grow from a thin strong blue stem and have such strong color, texture and line that they will please any flower arranger. They originated in the Alps and were cultivated in England as long ago as 1597. They now grow in any temperate area, producing their blue teasel-like heads of tiny flowers in late summer. They can be air-dried and will keep their color, so they are a very useful year-round flower for the arranger. We show off their ghostly luminous appearance by arranging them in an Art Nouveau vase (right) with a glaze that picks up the iridescent color of the stems. Loops of false pine leaves have been placed to follow through the design of the vase.

This arrangement uses a combination of shapes and sizes of flowers (left) reflected in the vase.
Plant material: *White Tulips, Liatrus, Ginistra, Iris, Queen Anne's Lace, Eucalyptus.*

The swirling rhythm of this composition (right) is suggested by the innately elegant design of the vase, while the steel blue of the sea holly and the green of the false palm is repeated in the striking glaze.
Plant materials: *Eryngium or Sea Holly, False Palm foliage.*

FOR A CHANGE

POT-ET-FLEURS

Busy people cannot always find time to enjoy and tend flower arranging but might choose to fill their homes with less time-consuming pot plants. The pot ferns and begonias grouped in the copper container here (below) will always look good even on their own but we demonstrate how, by slipping a narrow vase in between the plants to hold tall antirrhinums and a spray carnation, you can quickly transform a few pot plantsinto a coherent and arresting composition. Flowers can periodically be changed or renewed to restore the group to its former glory. An arrangement of pot plants and cut flowers combined in this way is called *Pot-et-Fleurs'*.

Pot-et-Fleurs *is the term used for pot plants and cut flowers grouped together. A glass coffee jar has been slipped between the plants in this handsome copper trough (below), and the flowers it holds give an extra height to the arrangement of plants, and can be changed from time to time to give a long-lasting but easy to maintain flower arrangement.* Plant materials: *Pot Ferns, Pot Begonias, Peach Spray Carnations, White Antirrhinum.*

The subtle combination of softly contrasted peach and pink shades (right) here enhances the fine harmony of the flowers, which are loosely placed and supported by an echoing combination of glass nuggets. The cylindrical glass vase allows these colors to fill the available space. Plant materials: *Carnations, Spray Carnations, Dahlias, Carnation foliage, Acaena foliage.*

GLASS NUGGETS

Most homes contain a variety of glass vases, but how often we discard them when arranging flowers for fear that the criss-cross stems of a mixed bunch will make the glass lose its attraction. This can be overcome by support-ing and hiding the stems using renewed glass nuggets. As these are manufactured in a wide selection of colored glass, you can also change the colors to match the flowers, as shown above and page 85. The reflective qualities of the glass give depth to the arrangement.

105

CHAMBER POT

The Victorians believed in decorating everything, including their chamber pots, and these highly decorated objects have now become prized collectors' items. They also happen to be a perfect shape for a mass arrangement that will be viewed from above. In the arrangement on page 112 we take the eye from the outline design decorating the pot by using a very positive blue mass of cornflowers to reflect the negative space of the design. The white carrot flower softens and breaks up the solid mass throughout the center.

FOLIAGE

There is not one week in the year when we cannot produce a selection of foliage covering the whole color range from yellows to bright greens, from cool silvers and grays to the warm yellows, purples and browns. Foliage is a very important part of any flower arrangement. The large variation in shades, the variety of leaf formations and shapes, provides the opportunity to make a foliage-only arrangement that will last very well and not need constant attention.

Florists stock a large selection. If you don't have a garden, it is worth remembering when buying flowers from your florist to buy at least half the quantity again of mixed foliage. These will give your flower arrangements a good background and shape and, as they usually last much longer than flowers, you will find gradually over the weeks that you have sufficient foliage to make several all-foliage arrangements which will fill up your home when you do not have time to buy fresh flowers.

All flower arrangers with gardens should develop an informal part of their garden where they cultivate trees, shrubs and herbs which will provide an all-year variety for them to cut. These should include plants with soft curly stems, such as honeysuckle, ivy and hops, and a variety of strong leathery shapes, for example camellia, laurel, holly and rhododendron. You will also need a selection of spiky grasses; these can be variegated or plain green, or from trees such as pine. The long blade-like leaves of iris are also very useful. Outline foliage which can be considered for arrangements includes beech, whitebeam, oak, laurel, box and privet. Large leaves suitable for focal points should be grown, such as hosta, magnolia, geranium, begonia and bergenia.

Good variegated foliages to include are dogwood, myrtle, privet and elaeagnus. Purple and red foliage is very useful for showing off flowers in pink arrangements; the most popular are smoke tree, purple beech, prunus, begonia and berberis. Among the silver foliages are all the artemisia, Jerusalem sage and sedum, while blue foliage includes eucalyptus, blue cedar and the very popular ruta (rue) called Jackman's blue.

Among soft fillers no garden should be without my very favorite flower, lady's mantle, seen in all its glory arranged on its own on page 17 and as used as a filler on page 54. Other useful fillers are the euphorbias, gypsophila and all the umbelliferae.

The combination shown right of curved and straight stems of foliage, variegated small and large leaves, with a focal point of green quince and green tomatoes, gives a very full three-dimensional effect for this tall all-round arrangement. Minimal green leaves and fruits have been used in the low arrangement on page 113. They have been arranged on a pin holder and placed off center in a bowl to make a design to be viewed from above.

When picked from the garden, all foliage should be stripped of its lower leaves, and the stems crushed and given a good twelve-hour drink in tepid water, preferably lying horizontal in a bath. After this leaves should be sponged clean and all damaged leaves pruned. Leathery leaves should be polished using a little mayonnaise to give a gloss to their appearance.

CONTAINERS

How often do we find the right container for our flowers only to discover that its wide neck means that the attractive bunch of flowers just collapses when placed on it. Overleaf we demonstrate how, with a criss-cross grid of sticky tape securely positioned over the top of the jug, the narrow opening will grip the flowers in position, allowing the beautiful shape of the jug to be displayed and giving full decorative value to the volume of water. Glass containers and vases are best reserved for clean stemmed flowers such as roses, gladioli, iris etc. The glass must always be scrupulously clean and the water changed regularly. A small piece of charcoal can be hidden behind some stems which will help to keep the water clear. The slightest discoloration of water or, worse still, sediment at the bottom of the vase will detract from the beauty of the arrangement and devalue the glass.

This long-lasting all-round arrangement (right) of an abundance of foliage has many shapes and textures. It suggests a harmony of greens that spill over the vase to direct the eye to the green shading in the orange pottery.

Plant materials: *Bells of Ireland, foliage of Boston Creeper, Cyclamen, Euonymus, Fern, Forsythia, Golden Privet, Hops, Iris, Kerria, Oak, Laurel, Pulmonaria, Sumach and Quinces and Tomatoes.*

106

Preparing Container for Arrangement

Using transparent adhesive tape, make a square grid across the top of the jug to reduce the area that will contain the flowers, securing the tape under the rim of the jug.

The lemon-like sharpness of yellow roses suggests summer drinks in the garden. A water jug makes a perfect vase for this occasion, but the wide neck of the jug has had to be narrowed, to support this casual bunch of garden flowers, by using sticky tape across the top of the jug to make a square grid, as illustrated below left. Plant materials: Yellow Roses, White Anthurium, Lobelia.

*These two arrangements show
how the overall shape of an
arrangement changes as tulips
open to their full perfection.
Plant materials: White Tulips,
Red Tulips.*

The dazzling effect of the blue of cornflowers can be quite breathtaking; here they are massed in an old Victorian chamber pot (below) that has a charming outline pattern of flowers and leaves. This draws the eye to the many delicately formed blue florets that make up each cornflower. The mass display has been broken up by a wavy pattern of heads of Queen Anne's Lace.
Plant materials: *Blue Cornflowers, Queen Anne's Lace.*

These early spring flowering shrubs and bulbs are arranged in an unusual container and weighted with stones. The forsythia will last a considerable time but the narcissi will need to be removed as they die.
Plant materials: *Forsythia, Narcissus.*

Champagne flutes make very good specimen vases for single stems of roses, freesia or jasmine; one placed in position for each dinner guest can result in a very attractive flower arrangement. A single camellia or a bunch of violets or primroses look delightful floating at the top of a brandy glass or goblet. A flat glass container allows the flowers and foliage to tip over the edge of the container and hide the stems which show through the glass, as seen on page 105.

A vase cupboard should contain a large assortment of shapes and sizes. They need not be expensive; but colored vases with a good shape can always be renewed with a matt spray. Some vases will only be of use once or twice a year, when a certain flower is available. The pearl-lacquered china cornucopia shown below can only hold lightweight flowers without over-balancing, and is always reserved for the beautiful shades of freesia or alstroemeria and grasses, which reflect the mauve tones in the pearlized container.

One of the pleasures of possessing a piece of china like the bowl illustrated on page 32 is knowing that at a certain time of year you can look forward to using the perfect

The feathery mixture of gray foliages create a soft outline for this all-round basket arrangement (left). The addition of pink flowers gives form and color to add to the delicacy of the pretty basket. This would make a welcome gift for a new-born baby girl.
Plant materials: *Pink Roses, White Stock, Pink Bouvardiar, Fresh Poppy seedheads, Artemisia foliage, Rock Rose foliage.*

The small branch of apple at the base (right) repeats the color and shape of the arrangement.
Plant materials: *Rubrum Lilies, Apple Blossom, Lemon Leaf.*

flowers to enhance the pattern of the dish. Pottery vases, besides holding plenty of water, have the weight to balance heavy branches and wide shapes. One can always make a tall vase shallower by placing bricks or sand up to a midway position, then gently lowering on top of this a container full of water, a jam jar or coffee jar, in which the flowers can be arranged.

Silver containers are not so popular for arranging flowers these days, although the beautiful delicate shapes of certain roses and freesia often seem to reflect all round the room if they are arranged in a silver bowl. Your imagination need know no bounds as regards china containers and the variety of shapes and colors available. You can have an endless collection of sauce boats, teapots, cups, egg cups, trinket boxes, jugs of all shapes and sizes, ink wells, sugar bowls, jam pots. You should always keep a lookout for good china shapes when in antique shops or at bric-á-brac sales to add to your collection.

Brass and copper containers come into their own in the autumn, when they enhance the golds and reds of the seasonal foliage and flowers. Wooden containers can always be lined with plastic film and filled with florist's foam, enabling you to use work boxes, knife boxes, candle boxes, cheese molds and fruit bowls. You can also line the many pretty and different shaped tins you may have collected over the years. One of my favorite items for lining in this way are baskets. Fresh flowers look wonderfully natural bursting from a handmade basket, and the arrangement shown above is the perfect indoor garden for a country cottage.

Dried Flowers
For
Everyday

I first became interested in dried flowers many years ago when I worked daily among flowers, arranging them in lovely London homes and special venues. While topping up and replacing flowers several times a week, I found I sometimes left in the arrangement seedheads, ferns, hydrangeas and larkspur, all of which dried quite naturally while retaining their color. These preserved seedheads and flowers mixed in well and allowed the financial savings to be put toward extra flower arrangements. This in turn led to experiments with many drying materials to produce large quantities of dried flowers to make arrangements to sell at my flower shop.

Gradually flower drying for that country living look became very popular, and imported Australian exotic flowers started to be incorporated. Then the popularity of dried flowers faded again over the years, with the advent of sharp colors and less formal flower arrangements. I was delighted when the Laura Ashley design movement brought back that country look in the late 1970s, which coincided with many growers giving over hundreds of acres to growing flowers for drying. The mid 1980s saw an enormous growth in the dried flower industry and dried flowers became readily available in stores, supermarkets and even on garage forecourts, while specialist shops opened selling large selections of flowers and foliages.

Flowers for drying are grown commercially in England, France, Italy, Australia, America and South Africa, though the center of the industry is situated in Holland, which exports billions of bunches of dried flowers daily, particularly to Austria where there is a tradition of making garlands of spices and nuts incorporating dried flowers. Holland also imports exotic flowers from America, Australia and Africa and repackages and re-exports to their worldwide market. The Dutch have researched and spent many millions of pounds on new improved methods for fast drying flowers. The flowers are picked, graded and bunched, and hung in rooms with air circulating at up to 60 degrees centigrade. This fast drying enables all the flowers to retain their color.

If you are buying dried flowers, find a specialist shop where they are interested in the flowers, and can tell you their names and advise on the handling and suitability of the various plant materials. Bunched flowers on display should be wrapped in either tissue or cellophane paper for protection. You will find that many imported flowers have been dyed and these can sometimes look quite garish and unacceptable; by carefully mixing them with natural colors, you can tone them down while giving depth to produce an almost fresh-looking display. There are some very exciting flowers and seedheads which are commonplace in Africa, Australia and North America and can give

interesting shape and an exciting focal point to your display. These can add depth to almost any dried flower arrangement. If you enjoy gardening, think what pleasure you can have if you can look at a beautiful arrangement of flowers that you have grown and dried from your own garden.

A popular easy-to-dry flower is the tall golden yarrow or achillea; lavenders also dry well, as do larkspur, roses, gypsophila and lady's mantle. You should grow a large collection of ornamental grasses; they dry beautifully and can add lightness to any dried flower arrangement. Seedheads are also plentiful and should be dried, as should bulrushes and the beautiful sprays of pampas. Fuller details about how to dry your flowers and grasses are given in the next chapter.

A hall would be the correct location for the fantastic mix of dried flowers in a basket shown here (right and detail overleaf). The basket was first filled with bricks to give weight to the arrangement and then the flowers were taken in small bunches and crammed into the basket, gradually building up height and giving a massed effect. Great care was taken to give the arrangement a flat back, so that it would fit tightly against a wall and, with its extra weight, would not be knocked over. This free-standing arrangement should give a great visual impact when anybody enters the hall.

ROSES

Roses are a very easy flower to dry, but do not use a multi-petaled variety. You should use roses that are just beginning to unfurl from their buds. The foliage should be removed and they should be tied in small bunches and hung in a very warm room with plenty of warm air circulating. The quicker they can be dried the better the color. Open roses can be dried in a desiccant (see page 158).

We have arranged peach roses in a classical creamware dish (page 122–123), breaking up the solidness of the shape by interspersing little bunches of quaking grass, giving a lovely peaches and cream effect. This arrangement would look beautiful in any room in the house. The pink roses on

This imposing arrangement of massed dried flowers would make a dramatic display for a hall. The mixture of shapes, textures and colors has been achieved by packing small bunches of single flowers tightly so that they flare out fan-fashion and fill the basket to capacity. Plant materials: Roses, *Hydrangea, Helichrysum, Love-in-a-Mist seedheads, Larkspur, Gypsophila, Love-Lies-Bleeding, Statice, Sea Lavender, Yarrow, Craspedia, Curry Plant, Golden Rod, Safflower, Sorrel, Reed Canary Grass, Reed Grass, Mugwort, Wattle, Sweet Chestnut foliage, Hair Grass, Broom Grass.*

Detail (below) of the massed flower arrangement on p 119.

The rich tone of these orange roses (right) is repeated in the brilliant color of the dimpled pottery vase and forms a contrast to the glycerined leaves which gives this arrangement impact. The orange dyed grass is interspersed to add graceful vertical proportions.
Plant materials: *Air-dried Orange Roses, dyed Timothy Grass, Glycerined Buddhist Pine.*

The open lacework of the classical creamware fruit bowl shields a block of florist's foam to hold this arrangement. The grasses flare out fan-shaped from the container and repeat the delicacy of the bowl's lacework. Form is added by the placement of each rose to complete this display of subtle harmony. Plant materials: *Briza Grass, Roses.*

page 124 have been arranged in a lovely antique cup and saucer. This little posy has been interspersed with pink strawflowers, bloom bloom and pressed fern, and would be ideal for a side table in a bedroom.

The more masculine arrangement of orange roses (page 121) demonstrates how well the roses work in pottery; here they are mixed with glycerined Buddhist pine and Timothy grass that has been dyed orange. The massed red roses (right) have been interspersed with baby's breath gypsophila and tipped into a beautiful old rustic basket.

Small mixed posies of dried flowers can be charming, particularly if the flowers have been carefully dried in desiccant. In the arrangement illustrated on pages 126-130, the pompom white-edged dahlias are interspersed with desiccant-dried estrantia and white status. The handsome basket on page 132 is another beautiful mix of textures, and care was taken not to cover up any part of this basket. By cutting all the dried material short and arranging it in a dome shape, both basket and plant material are seen at their best. This arrangement is suitable for placing low

This light all-round posy of mixed dried flowers (below) is appropriate to the delicate design of the antique cup and saucer. It would make a pretty display for a side table, as it can be viewed from all sides. Small dried or fresh flowers give an excellent opportunity to remove decorative cups and saucers from a display cabinet and allow them to be viewed to full advantage.
Plant materials: *Pink dried Roses, Helichrysum, Sneezewort, Broom Bloom and pressed Maidenhair Fern.*

This extravagantly simple design (right) relies on an abundance of red roses to provide the main interest. They have been massed into a rustic woven basket, while the delicate blossoms of white gypsophila give contrast to the color and form of the roses.
Plant materials: *Red Roses, Gypsophila Baby's Breath.*

This simple dried arrangement can be sewn on top of a basket which would then be suitable for holding pot pourri or dried lavender.
Plant material: *Lavendar, Lamb's Ears.*

126

It takes more than a second glance to confirm that this exquisite miniature arrangement is made of dried flowers. The pretty posy bowl contains foam to support the stems of this all-round loose posy.

Plant materials: *Pom Pom Dahlias, Astrantia, Statice, Pressed Maidenhair Fern, Grass, Larkspur.*

127

down or even free standing on a floor or in a fireplace.

The more highly colored arrangement on page 131 would brighten up any corner in a lounge. The beautiful glaze and pattern on the pottery container has been carefully picked up by the choice of materials. The blue-gray glycerined eucalyptus leaves and the blue of the larkspur contrast with the focal point and strength in the center of the arrangement given by the golden yarrow. Again this vase was weighted down with sand to make sure it could not be tipped over.

Step by step instructions for arrangement on pages 126-127

1. Place a one-inch layer of silica gel in a plastic box. Cut pom pom dahlias short and replace stems with stub wire.

2. Place the dahlias on the desiccant in straight lines, making sure they do not touch. Using a spoon, carefully cover all the dahlias until they have a covering of about an inch. Seal with lid and place in a warm cupboard.

3. *After five days remove the lid from the box and gradually shake out the desiccant. Carefully remove the flowers and use a paint brush to brush out any remaining desiccant. Cover the wires in stem tape.*

4. *Fill the posy bowl with foam and position pressed maidenhair fern to make an all-round outline. Position mixed flowers to make a very pretty display.*

This graceful vertical arrangement (right) has been established in a strong base. The vigorous combination of silver, blue and gold shades is accentuated by the irregular placement of the flowers. These have been carefully chosen to reflect the glaze of the pottery base, while the strong color and texture of the yellow yarrow is placed in opposition to the dominant design on the vase. Plant materials: glycerined Eucalyptus, dried Larkspur, dried Golden Yarrow.

130

An occasional table would be an ideal position to place the little basket of flowers shown below and overleaf. This good all-round design can be viewed from any position and would look ideal placed on a coffee table and viewed from above. The dark leaves used to outline the design give it great depth, while the textured handle gives it a pleasing visual appearance.

This handsome textured basket (left) was first filled with tightly packed hydrangea heads, which were allowed to rest at the rim of the basket. The strong vertical lines of this container were echoed by positioning short stems of dyed oats. These were then interspersed with dried poppy heads and artificial fruits to make a display to be viewed from above. This would make a perfect fireplace display.
Plant materials: Hydrangea, maroon dyed Oats, Poppy seedheads, artificial fruits.

A base of dark glycerined magnolia leaves gives the basket of mixed peach dried flowers on page 137 depth and texture. The dark tones are repeated throughout the design by interspersing glycerined wattle foliage to complete this delightful gift. Step-by-step instructions follow.
Plant materials: *Helichrysum, Gypsophila, Broom Bloom, Larkspur, Roses, dried Love-in-a-Mist seed pods, glycerined Magnolia leaves, glycerined Wattle foliage.*

Step by step instructions
1. Stick pieces of adhesive tape to plastic pin holders and secure at bottom of basket. Shape a piece of florist's foam to fit basket and impale on plastic pin holders.

2. Using black reel wire, wire ends of foliage and push into foam to make a base around the rim of basket.

*3. Cut larkspur short and
arrange this between the foliage.
Gradually fill in with roses,
helichrysum and groups of love-
in-a-mist seed pods.*

4. Wire together small bunches of bleached broom bloom and use these to fill in the gaps in the basket.

DRIED FLOWERS
FOR
SPECIAL OCCASIONS

Although most brides carry fresh flowers on the day of their wedding, a choice of dried flowers for the bouquet will mean that the bride will have a lasting keepsake. As dried flowers can be rather brittle, however, it is important to arrange either a posy or a tightly packed 'shower' bouquet. This mixture of pale to deeper pinks (below) is highlighted by using roses and peonies as a focal point of the bouquet. A coronet could be made for the bride using the same flowers, and small posies or baskets could be made for the bridesmaids, while the smaller flowers of the bouquet could be used for decorating the cake, and swags could be made to decorate the church. The candle designs (right) would make a lovely arrangement for the reception table, while the bride's mother would look in keeping if

Practical as well as fashionable, this tear-drop-shaped dried wedding bouquet (left) will remain a lasting memento for the bride. The peonies and roses are wired in tight groups to give form, while the larkspur and eucalyptus leaves give line and movement. The graduating shades of pink blend harmoniously together.
Plant materials: *Roses, Peonies, Larkspur, Gypsophila, Hair Grass, Snow Gum, Eucalyptus leaves.*

The soft shades of peach flowers rest in a graceful lateral position and give height to this arrangement (right), suitable for a buffet table. A block of dried foam is secured to the top of the candlestick and the candle is pushed through this into the holder, allowing the plant material to be positioned in a display of extreme delicacy.
Plant materials: *Helichrysum, dyed Quaking Grass, Yarrow, dyed Rabbit's Tail Grass, artificial turquoise leaves to match candlestick.*

Resembling a carved Roman swag, this harvest garland (left) is created using a combination of dried and glycerined materials giving the merest suggestion of curve. The mixture of shapes and textures is backed by glycerined oak leaves. This design can be repeated using mixed dried flowers and bows to make pew ends for the bride who will carry a dried bouquet. Step-by-step instructions follow on pages 144-147.

Plant materials: *Barley, Miniature Bulrushes, Quaking Grass, Crab Apples, Corn on the Cob, Artichoke, glycerined Oak leaves.*

her hat were decorated with dried flowers as the hat shown below. She could also use the hat afterwards as a wall decoration.

Weddings are not the only time of the year to use dried flowers for celebrations. The harvest swag (left), also illustrated in the step-by-step arrangements, can be made up in different colors to use as a Christmas swag, incorporating red ribbons, green foliage and berries. Alternatively similar flowers to the bride's could be used to make this a pew-end arrangement for a wedding. How nice to deck a copper bowl at Thanksgiving time by using dried fungus and sorrel, hair grass and the exotic Australian honeysuckle.

Lightening a black straw hat (below), to create a festive wedding decoration, the combination of mixed peach dried flowers makes a stunning addition to transform a hat for that all important occasion. A crescent shape of broom bloom establishes a foundation, while the positioning of roses and soft black rabbit's ear grass adds texture and shape.

Plant materials: *Broom Bloom, Roses, dyed black Rabbit's Ear Grass.*

Step by step instructions

1. Take a piece of wood about one inch wide and six inches long. Using black reel wire, secure a loop near the top, then cover this with brown stem tape.

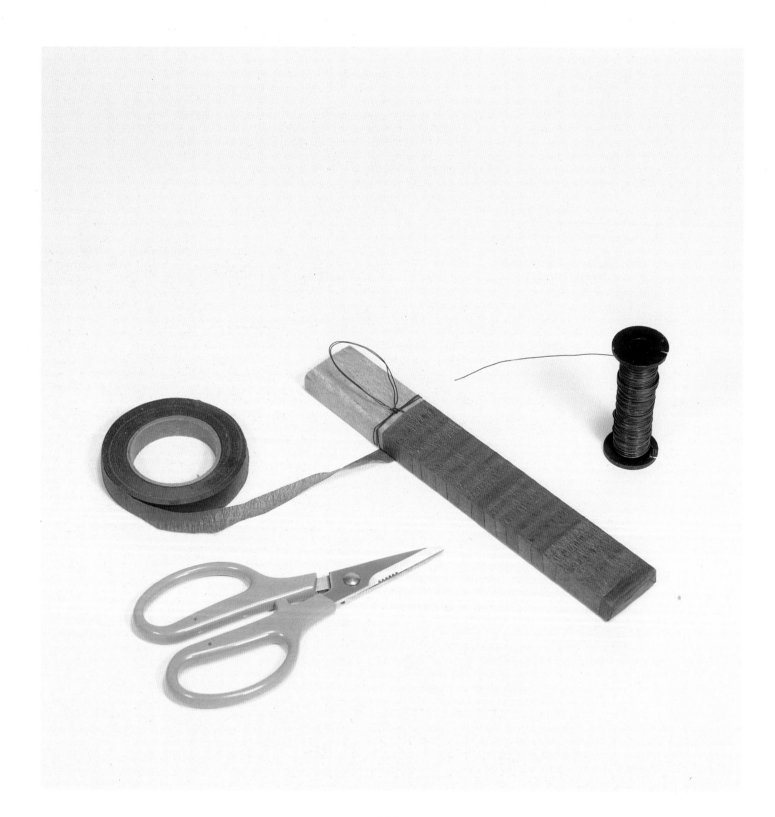

2. Take the mixed plant materials, cut them short and, using black reel wire, wire them into groups.

3. Prepare a paper bow, gold spray some of the groups of corn that will add highlights to the display, then take some oak leaves, corn and rushes and bind together to form the tail of the swag.

4. Bind this tail to the wooden base, then gradually bind in more foliage along each side and fill in the center with the mixed material until it is covered. Finish with the bow and place the artichokes in the center.

For a seasonal celebration a foam ring is dressed for a Hallowe'en or Thanksgiving Party by using Chinese lanterns and orange and black bows. The skeletonized leaves build a cobwebby outer edge, while in the center their tips point toward the flames of the Hallowe'en candles. This design can be repeated for Easter by using yellow candles, green and yellow bows, foliage and small Easter eggs to decorate the wreath. For Christmas, red or white candles could be used, while green and red bows, pine cones and holly berries, could decorate the base.

Plant materials: *Chinese lanterns, skeletonized Magnolia leaves, black dyed Yarrow, black dyed Oats and foliage.*

Hallowe'en is an exciting time to make a piece for the table, as in the step-by-step illustrations on how to make the arrangement left. This is another all seasons design; if yellow candles are used, with yellow bows and green foliage and assorted Easter eggs, it could look beautiful as a table center at Easter time. At Christmas you can use red, green or white candles and fill the center wreath with cones and foliage, berries and baubles on red and green bows.

Step by step instructions

1. Insert five candle holders into a foam wreath, then spray the skeletonized leaves and mixed foliage with black spray paint.

149

2. Using black reel wire, wire groups of grasses together.

3. Push the skeletonized leaves into the outside edge of the foam ring between two candle cups, then make a cluster of the mixed black grasses and flowers. Next position the individual Chinese lanterns. Keep this grouping between the candle cups.

4. Using short lengths of paper ribbon, wire together to make small bows. Add the bows to each grouping. Finally add the candles.

This arrangement (right) has found a different use for an antique copper colander. The daisy shapes in the center are highlighted by bleached grasses and the black-eared barley adds drama and height, while Dudinea seedheads are positioned to spill over the edge, adding color reflection.

Plant materials: Black-eared Barley, Reed Grass, Dudinea, Safflower, Protea.

Using the same containers for several different arrangements can be very interesting. In this arrangement (right) we have used straight-sided green pottery vases and kept all the flowers to shades of red. They make a very nice arrangement viewed as a complete display, or each one could be used individually. Dried flowers can be arranged in almost anything, as we demonstrate by lining a small copper colander and filling it with dried oasis (see page 153), then making an arrangement of mixed creams to browns. The Greek pot on page 156 has a very small opening, which dictated the material we could use; the multi-branched stems of eucalyptus give a soft, rounded arrangement that matches the pot, and the color of the terracotta is picked up in the bunches of gundea.

DRYING YOUR FLOWERS

Unlike fresh flowers, flowers for drying must only be picked on a dry day, at about midday, as soon as the dew has dried and the sap is rising. They must be in optimum condition, preferably before pollination has taken place. If you do pick on a damp day, gently shake the flowers free of water and place them in a container with about an inch of water, leaving the stems to dry off. Remember also to collect the grasses and seedheads before they start to rattle. The drying process will take some time, so only pick sufficient for the time you have allowed.

AIR DRYING

There are two main methods of air drying. With the upside down method, you need to fix a line or pole across an airy dark room, where you can leave the flowers for some time while they are drying. Strip all the foliage from the flowers, arrange the heads at various levels and secure the ends of the bunch with rubber bands. Use a wire bent in an 'S' hook to hang the bunches head down from the line in your room. Do not crowd too many flowers into each bunch or crowd them on the line. Leave the air to circulate and carry on the dehydration process. Keeping the room dark will help retain the color of the flowers.

Grasses, sea lavender, Chinese lanterns, statice and bulrushes are best dried in an upright position, placed in a base of dried sand or dry florist's foam. Lady's mantle and Queen Anne's lace should be started by hanging upside down, and transferred to the upright position when nearly dry so they can dry in a more natural shape. Heavy seedheads like globe artichokes and corn on the cob need support and extra space while drying. You can achieve this by stretching a piece of wire mesh or netting over a wooden frame or box top, putting this in a warm place and placing the stems through the mesh so that the netting holds the head.

A festival wreath for a door can be made from dried foliage and dried flowers, trimmed with ribbon, and can remain in place long after Christmas without looking unseasonal (below).
Plant materials: *Eucalyptus, Russian Statice, Lemon Leaves, Larkspur, Dried Roses.*

You can create an unusual Christmas tree (right) by wiring ornamental dried grass to a wire frame, adding gypsophila, and trimming with gilt ornaments and lights.
Plant materials: *Ornamental Dried Grass, Gypsophila Baby's Breath.*

Rosebuds wired to a heart-shaped frame and tied with a ribbon (left) give a typically country look and add a hint of color to walls, doors or windows.
Plant materials: *Dried Rosebuds.*

Harvest colors are reflected in this antique and beautifully polished copper water carrier (below). The soft bronze briza grass establishes the principal contours of the pattern, while the dominant stems of Australian honeysuckle give a lustrous richness and contrast with the dried fungus, symbolizing autumn.
Plant materials: *Reed Grass, Briza Segromi Grass, Australian Honeysuckle, dried Fungus.*

You should hang large delphinium and bells of Ireland stems singly for drying. Helichrysum required for use as a single head should be wired after picking and before drying. Helichrysum dried on stems with some of the top foliage left can be gathered up into a simple but quick hand bunch arrangement.

DRYING IN WATER

When hydrangea and yarrow start to become crisp pick them and bring them indoors to protect them from the weather. Place them in a container of suitable height, with one inch of water in the base, and allow them to drink themselves dry. These two are among the most durable dried flowers.

USING A DESICCANT

A desiccant is a material that will readily take up moisture from other materials placed near it. The ones most commonly used for drying flowers include borax, detergent powder, silica gel and silver sand. Borax powder is perfect for fine petals and can be dried and reused, but it is sometimes difficult to brush off the finer parts of the flower. Detergent powder will dry small and larger flowers and should only be used once; like borax it can sometimes stick to the petals. Silica gel is the most expensive, but also the quickest and best desiccant. It can be dried out between use and used time and time again. It can be used with all sizes of flower; crystals can be ground down in a liquidizer or coffee grinder to a very fine powder and will dry even the smallest flower, enabling you to keep their shape. Silver sand works well with thicker petals and plant material, but it is slow acting, taking up to three weeks, and may not remove the last traces of moisture.

Use a large plastic box with an airtight lid, for instance a two or four liter ice cream container. Place a layer of dried-out desiccant at the base of the box, cut the stems short, to within half an inch of the flowers, and attach a wire. Carefully lay the flowers in the desiccant, making sure they do not touch. Using a spoon, slowly sprinkle more desiccant in among the petals and continue until they are covered by about one inch of the desiccant, then seal the lid. Inspect the flowers after a few days; they are ready when they are dry and paper, but not too papery. With silica gel this might take two to four days. If left too long the flowers dry too much and become too fragile to handle. Carefully pour the desiccant into another container and pick out the flowers one at a time as they come to the surface. Lay them aside on a tray. When you have removed them all, carefully brush off the last remains of the desiccant adhering to the flowers with an artist's soft paintbrush, then turn them upside down on a soft folded muslin and cover the wires with stem tape. The pompom dahlias on page 127, with their tightly packed petals, took four days to dry in silica gel.

GLYCERINE

Glycerine is mostly used for preserving foliage. It will change the colors to shades of brown but the foliage will retain its suppleness and three-dimensional appearance, and unlike dried material is not easily damaged. Once preserved, foliage has a double use, both with dried flowers and also with fresh flowers where it will no longer take up water. Make a mixture of 60% glycerine and 40% hot water. Pour it into a glass jar, put the jar in the center of a large container, such as a bucket. Strip off the lower foliage, scrape away the bark off the bottom two inches of the stem, crush the ends with a hammer and put the stems to be preserved in the jar, using the bucket rim to support the foliage. Depending on the foliage type it will take between one and four weeks to preserve it. You will be able to tell from the color and feel of the leaves when it is ready.

To glycerine individual leaves use a 50-50 mixture, place leaves in a shallow dish and cover with the solution. Push the leaves down into the mixture from time to time. They should be ready in a few days, then lift them out and wash out in a soapy mixture, put on folded newspaper and pat dry.

This monochrome arrangement illustrates the subtle harmony of dried flowers, here established in a strong base provided by a converted fender. The shape of each preserved peony blossom invites attention, as they stand erect in this imitation of a garden border, and the whole would make a very handsome display in a fireplace.
Plant materials: *Larkspur, Roses, Peonies, Foliage and Lichen.*

Botanical names of popular flowers

ARTEMISIA *Artemisia abrotanum*
ANTIRRHINUM *Antirrhinum majus*
ANEMONE (JAPANESE) *Anemone hupehensis*
AGAPANTHUS *Agapanthus campanulatis*
ALSTROEMERIA *Alstroemeria ligtu hybds.*
ARTICHOKE (GLOBE) *Cynara scolymus*
ASTRANTIA *Astrantia major*
AFRICAN DAISY *Dimorphotheca calendulacea*
AUSTRALIAN HONEYSUCKLE *Banksia menzieii*
ASTERS *Callistephus chinensis*
ALPINE ALCHEMILLA MOLLIS
  FOLIAGE *Alchemilla erigena*
APPLES *Malus*
ALCHEMILLA *Alchemilla mollis*

BELLS OF IRELAND *Molucella laevis*
BASIL *Ocimum basilicum*
BUDDLEIA *Buddleia fallowiana*
BEGONIAS (POT) *Begonia*
BOUVARDIA *Bouvardia domestica*
GLYCERINED BUDDHIST PINE *Podocarpus macrophyllus*
BROME GRASS *Bromus sp.*
BRIZA GRASS *Briza maxima*
BIRDS NEST FERN *Asplenium nidus*
BROOM BLOOM *Laspana communis*
BARLEY (BLACKEARED) *Hordeum sp.*
MINIATURE BULRUSHES (LESSER
  REEDMACE) *Typha angustifolia*
BROOM *Cytisus*
BANKSIA *Banksia menzieii*

CLEMATIS *Clematis*
CHRYSANTHEMUMS (YELLOW SPRAY
  SPIDER) *Chrysanthemum*
CHOISYA FOLIAGE *Choisya ternata*
CAMOMILE *Anthriscus nobilis*
CORNFLOWERS (BLUE) *Centaurea cyanus*
COTONEASTER FOLIAGE *Cotoneaster horizontalis*
CROTON FOLIAGE *Codiaeum reidii*
CARNATIONS (SPRAY) *Dianthus caryophyllus*
CYMBIDIUM (PIEDMONT) *Cymbidium alexanderi*
PURPLE DECORATIVE CABBAGE *Brassica*
CRASPEDIA *Craspedia globosa*
CURRY PLANT *Helichrysum angustifolium*
CANTERBURY BELLS *Campanula medium*
CHINESE FOLIAGE *Polyscias fruticosa*
CYCLAMEN *Cyclamen persicum*
CARNATION FOLIAGE *Dianthus*
CRAB APPLES *Malus x lemoinei*
CORN ON THE COB *Zea mays*
CHINESE LANTERNS *Physalis alkekengi franchetii*
CUPRESSUS *Cupressus*

DUDINEA SEED HEADS *Dudinea*
DILL *Anethum graveolens*
DAISIES *Bellis perennis*
DAHLIAS *Dahlia*
DOGWOOD *Cornus alba*

ECHINOPS LEAVES *Echinops ritro*
EASTER LILIES *Lilium longiflorum*
EUONYMUS *Euonymus japonicus*
EUCALYPTUS *Eucalyptus cinera*

FREESIAS *Freesia hybs.*
FEVERFEW *Chrysanthemum parthenium*
FALSE PALM LEAVES *Cordyline terminala*

FORSYTHIA *Forsythia x intermedia*
FERN (BOSTON) *Nephrolepis exaltata bostoniensis*

GLADIOLI (MINIATURE) *Gladiolus x hortulanus hybs.*
GYPSOPHILA *Gypsophila paniculata*
GERBERA *Gerbera jamesonii*
GOLDEN ROD *x solidaster luteus*
GRAPES *Vitis*
GOLDEN PRIVET *Ligustrum ovalipolium*

HEUCHERA (PALACE PURPLE) *Heuchera americana*
HYDRANGEA *Hydrangea macrophylla*
HELICHRYSUM *Helichrysum bracteatum*
HAIR GRASS *Aira sp.*
HOLLYHOCKS *Althaea*
HEATHER *Ericaceae*
HOPS *Humulus lupulus*
HONEYSUCKLE *Lonicera periclymenum serotina*
HEBE *Veronica hebe gdn hybs.*
HOLLY *Ilex aquifolium*

IRIS FOLIAGE *Iris germanica*
IRIS *Iris x hollandica hybs.*
IVY *Hedera helix*

JAPONICA (FLOWERING QUINCE) *Chaenomeles x superba*

KERRIA *Kerria japonica*

LOVE-LIES-BLEEDING *Amaranthus caudatus*
LAVENDER *Lavandula officinalis*
LOVE-IN-A-MIST *Nigella damascena*
LOBELIA *Lobelia erinus*
LARKSPUR *Delphinium ajacis*
LADY'S MANTLE *Alchemilla mollis*
LADY'S MANTLE FOLIAGE *Alchemilla erigena*
LICHEN *Cladonia sp.*
LILY OF THE VALLEY *Convallaria majalis*
LAURUSTINUS *Viburnum tinus*
LILY *Lilium*
LAUREL *Prunus laurocerasus*
LILY BLUE AFRICAN *Agapanthus campanulatis*

MAGNOLIA *Magnolia*
MAIDENHAIR FERN *Adiantum cuneatum*
MARGUERITE *Argyrantheum frutescens*
MEADOW FOXTAIL GRASS *Alopecurus pratensis*
MUGWORT *Artemisia vulgaris*
MICHAELMAS DAISY *Aster novae-angliae*
MALLOW *Malva alcea*
MYRTLE *Myrtus communis*

NIPPLEWORT *Laspana communis*

ORIGANUM *Origanum marjorana*
OAK *Quercus robur*
OATS (MAROON DYED) *Avena fatua*

PANSIES (MAUVE) *Viola*
PLUMS *Prunus domestica*
PROTEA *Protea sp.*
POPPY SEED HEADS *Papaver somniferum*
PINKS *Dianthus plumarius*
PAEONY *Paeonia*

PINE *Picea abies*
PULMONARIA *Pulmonaria angustifolia*

QUEEN ANNE'S LACE (WILD
  CHERVIL) *Chaerophyllum temulentum*
QUAKING GRASS *Briza maxima*

ROCK ROSE FOLIAGE *Cistus x cyprius*
ROSES *Rosa hybs.*
ROSEMARY *Rosmarinus officinalis*
REED CANARY GRASS *Phalaris arundinacea*
REED SWEET GRASS *Glyceria maxima*
RABBITS TAIL GRASS *Phleum alpinum*
ROSEHIPS *Rosa canina*
RUSCUS FOLIAGE *Ruscus aculeatus*

SNAPDRAGON *Antirrhinum majus*
SPIRAEA *Spiraea arguta*
SAGE *Salvia officinalis*
SOUTHERN WOOD *Artemisia abrotanum*
SCABIOUS *Scabious atropurpurea*
SALVIA *Salvia nemorosa*
SNEEZEWORT *Achillea ptarmica*
SWEET PEAS *Lathyrus odoratus*
STOCKS *Matthiola incana*
SEA LAVENDER *Limonium tataricum*
SAFFLOWER *Carthamus tinctorius*
SORREL *Sorrel acetosa*
SWEET CHESTNUT FOLIAGE *Castanea sativa*
STATICE *Limonium sinuatum*
STRELITZIA (BIRD OF PARADISE) *Strelitzia*
SUMMER SNOW *Physostegia virginiana*
SNOWGUM *Eucalyptus niphophila*
SPATHIPHYLLUM *Spathiphyllum*
SPRUCE (BLUE) *Picea pungens*
SUMACH *Sumach typhina*
SEA HOLLY *Eryngium planum*

TIMOTHY GRASS *Phleum pratense*
TUBEROSE *Polianthes tuberosa*
THISTLE *Eryngium*
TOBACCO PLANT *Nicotiana alata*
THYME *Thymus*
THROATWORT (BLUE) *Trachelium caeruleum*

WATTLE *Acacia sp.*
WHITE POPLAR *Populus alba*

YARROW *Achillea filipendulina*

VERONICA *Hebe albicans*
VERBENA *Verbena bonariensis*

Acknowledgments

The author and publisher would like to thank the following for supplying materials: candles by Candlewick Green, London; glass nuggets and glass vase by Teign Valley Glass, Bovey Tracey; wedding cake by Newsteads Bakeries Ltd, Ipswich; garden produce by Mr Gordon Pett and Mrs G A Seinet; other materials from the author's gallery, Swan Craft Gallery, Ashfield-cum-Thorpe, Suffolk.